# The History of Early Medieval Towns of North and Central Italy

## The contribution of archaeological evidence

Giacomo Gonella

BAR International Series 1780
2008

Published in 2016 by
BAR Publishing, Oxford

BAR International Series 1780

*The History of Early Medieval Towns of North and Central Italy*

ISBN  978 1 4073 0268 3

BAR Publishing is the trading name of British Archaeological Reports (Oxford) Ltd.
British Archaeological Reports was first incorporated in 1974 to publish the BAR
Series, International and British. In 1992 Hadrian Books Ltd became part of the BAR
group. This volume was originally published by Archaeopress in conjunction with
British Archaeological Reports (Oxford) Ltd / Hadrian Books Ltd, the Series principal
publisher, in 2008. This present volume is published by BAR Publishing, 2016.

Printed in England

# BAR
PUBLISHING

BAR titles are available from:

        BAR Publishing
        122 Banbury Rd, Oxford, OX2 7BP, UK
EMAIL   info@barpublishing.com
PHONE  +44 (0)1865 310431
  FAX  +44 (0)1865 316916
        www.barpublishing.com

## Acknowledgements

*My grateful thanks to Prof. Guido Vannini for reading through and commenting; to Prof. Andrea Zorzi for encouraging me; to Dr. Stefano Roascio and Dr. Aurora Cagnana for interesting suggestions. I am finally thankful to Dr. Michele Nucciotti and Dr. Francesca Cheli for helping with the formatting of text and illustrations.*

*My special thanks to David Davison for this opportunity to publish within British Archaeological Reports.*

# Contents

# Introduction

This work is a *status quaestionis* of the research and the knowledge of the Early Medieval town in Italy.[1]

The chronological and geographical limits of this analysis (the regions of Central and Northern Italy between Late Antiquity, c. 4th-5th century, and the end of the Early Middle Ages, c. 10th-11th century)[2] have been selected on the basis of the changes and the solutions that emerged for political, economic, and social aspects, as a consequence of a succession of events that occurred earlier and in a more conclusive way in such contexts, trying then to point out eventual developments until the phases that precede the time of the city-states.

For these reasons too, scholars have turned a particular attention to this area of study, a fact which has in this sense produced an increase of excavations, with a tendency (even though not always quickly accomplished) to optimize the survey both in its archaeological elaboration[3] and in its interaction within wider historical problems: the intent of this work is to carry out a critical analysis of the available research-data, of scholars' interpretations and also of those circumstances in which material finds have allowed a comparison with, or a review of, the literary sources concerned.[4]

Over the last twenty years, in concomitance with the increase of archaeological data of a certain importance, the considerable interest especially in the transition-times between Late Antiquity and the Early Middle Ages has started a lively debate which, amongst the more "pessimistic" conclusions, has even denied the existence of a real urbanism throughout the aforesaid centuries:[5] Such a critical position actually comes from a strict comparison with the Augustan town (marble-),

which, however, does not seem to fully attest to reality as early as the Tetrarchic Age, when, after the end of the military anarchy, certain political and economic measures began to be taken, a fact that will have further marked the subsequent development of towns and territory too.[6]

The ancient model must doubtlessly be considered for better understanding the possible developing lines, but, on the other hand, it would be anachronistic (and misleading) to judge far later situations by standards peculiar to the Republican or early Roman Imperial times, since each age can be notably characterised by different problems as well as by a different concept of the urban centre itself:[7] far from representing an excuse for medievalists, this fact should rather be an incentive to find out the causes which brought about the changes of the transition-centuries and then to stress if (and to what extent) towns do show, in their Late Antique and Early Medieval phases, those features properly considered as urban at that time (this truly marking their "success" or "failure").[8]

Scholars seem to have aimed at this research purpose in recent years, without straining their results necessarily towards one of the two well-known interpretative views, that of "break" and that of a kind of "continuity": the *Brescia* and *Verona* patterns arose, in fact, from the intent, in the mid-eighties, to first outline the features of the Early Medieval towns on the basis of convincing archaeological evidence, starting, nevertheless, from still incomplete matches and from a too limited geographical area, whilst only a slightly less fragmentary picture was not achieved before the following decade.[9]

---

[1] This work is based on the final dissertation concerning the graduation in Medieval Archaeology of this writer (*"Il contributo dell'archeologia alla storia della città altomedievale. Italia centro-settentrionale"*, achieved at the University of Florence on July the 15th 2003; supervisor Professor Guido Vannini, Medieval Archaeology; examiner Professor Andrea Zorzi, Medieval History; co-examiner Professor Giovanni Cherubini, Medieval History), reviewed and updated for this publication.
[2] A certain attention is however turned to southern Italy too, as much for an essential comparison as for some similar junctures (i.e., the presence of Longobards also in those regions).
[3] A complete (and not common) interdisciplinary collaboration emerges from the work on Genoa edited by Dr. Melli (see references).
[4] For example, if the famous *versus Mediolanensis*, 739 AD, which, describing Milan on the basis of a classical model, does not seem to be correct about the paving at least (Wickham 1994, p.746), the Papyrus *Tjaeder* gives an irreplaceable pattern as to reconstructing some building typologies of Early Medieval Ravenna (and also of other contexts).
[5] Brogiolo-Gelichi 1998, p.13 and following, deals with this subject exhaustively.

[6] To the 3rd century is dated the early abandonment of several *domus* (especially in the north-east of the peninsula, because of the first barbarian raids; cf. chap.2, note 70), as well as the process of privatising some public areas (as pointed out for Tuscany; cf. chap.2, note 68): these courses mark big changes, to be referred to the new steps generally taken as regards the organization of territorial defence and control (particularly evident in the diverse distribution of the resources, in a certain militarization of the society and in the state control of some kinds of production, like the 4th century factories: cf. chapter 1st final remarks).
[7] Ward-Perkins 1996, p.4 and following; also Wickham 1994, p.742.
[8] Brescia and Milan, for example, can be considered as "winning" cities, but only in the light of Early Medieval planning and structures (La Rocca 1994, p.550), whilst they would not have been recognizable for an ancient Roman (Wickham 1994, p.745); in this sense can be seen the distinction between "the successful and the unsuccessful towns" pointed out by Arthur-Patterson 1994, pp.412-423, as regards Central and South Italy.
[9] References here concerned can be Brogiolo 1987, pp.27-46 (about Brescia) and La Rocca 1986, pp.31-78 (about Verona).

The considerable increase of material data throughout the last twenty years can be immediately noted, for instance, in the *status quaestionis* (of the analytical research in this sense) done by Ward Perkins in 1983, compared with that carried out by Wickham in 1999,[10] which shows definite positive progress, and has allowed a clearer focus on some of the most important urban characteristics, especially relevant to the transition between Late Antiquity and the Early Medieval time, a period "of particularly radical change in urban forms and functions".[11]

The regions of Central and Northern Italy were the first ones to be stricken, though to different extents, by a series of events (especially war) by which, on one hand, the northernmost areas went back again to their border role as early as the 3rd century, on the other hand, new organizational features became necessary earlier, in order to control territory and manage production and resources (as well as distribution).[12] Without dwelling on problems to deal further with, let us note that this is the key point to understanding those social-economic evolutions and devolutions that will have subsequently interested also other areas of the peninsula, especially in concomitance with wider occurrences (the Greek-Gothic war, Longobard invasion; relevant to commerce, the Vandal conquest of Africa too may be warily remembered).[13]

For a more complete analysis, nevertheless, cultural and "ideological" changes must be considered at the same time, in which both the coming of foreign people and Christianisation had a share, this being certainly one of the most peculiar aspects of the time here considered: the ecclesiastical institution, a sound presence since the 5th century, interacted in a conclusive way with a fact sometimes interpreted as sign of degradation, that of urban burials,[14] whilst it played a fundamental role in assimilating and "homogenising" different customs and traditions (a clear example is its relationship with the Longobards[15]); finally, it also represented, through its organizational structures (for instance, monasteries), an active element in the recovery of town and territory production-systems, beginning from about the 8th century.[16]

A kind of cultural change is at times assumed, yet regarding new building typologies, especially wood (the longhouses at Luni; the widespread sunken huts[17]), which, if they certainly show a foreign influence – there

are strict comparisons with contexts beyond the Alps – largely seem to derive from social and economic causes too.[18]

Furthermore, just concerning economic factors, a last remark can be made, to be rather considered as a possible research subject, since it does not appear to be supported by any clear archaeological evidence, at least until the end of the Early Middle Ages.

Apart from more immediate events (political, military, etc.), productive systems and, in particular, trading might have reached saturation point by the end of the 2nd and the beginning of the 3rd century (relevant, for instance, to that natural "crisis cycle" of Lucca at that time),[19] involving therefore an interaction of those market laws which, however, run their course even far above contemporaries' awareness:[20] in light of this, could be admitted a progressive devolution of the exchanges (lasting further into the following centuries),[21] whose distribution network might have been undermined at the base; on the contrary, the continued persistence of some trades much later, pointed out especially in some regions of Central and Southern Italy,[22] would be consequently considered as aftermaths of former structures, going through usual routes and ways.

A "fresh" demand and new markets would have represented, at that point, the only way out of an economic recession or slump and, in relation to such a matter, should be weighed up those innovative elements that developed and strengthened throughout the central centuries of the Early Middle Ages: on the one hand, the coming of the Arabs on the scene, on the other, the consolidation of the Frankish Kingdom as well as of political-administrative and organizational structures generally in North Europe.

This is far from being a support of Pirenne's well-known theory – moreover based on luxury-commodities-exchanges, which never weigh heavily upon the market[23] – being firmly persuaded, in fact, that the prosperity of regions such as those of the Po Valley would have rather

---

[10] Ward Perkins 1983, pp.111-124; Wickham 1999, pp.1-10.

[11] Christie-Loseby 1996, p.1.

[12] Brogiolo-Gelichi 1998, p.59.

[13] For an analysis of eventual "break-points", especially about trading, throughout the ages concerned, cf. Wickham 1999, p.2 and following.

[14] For this question see Brogiolo-Gelichi 1998, p.100.

[15] It could be thought to the royal and noble burials inside religious buildings as well as to the change of Lombards' funerary custom; Lusuardi Siena-Giostra-Spalla 2000 (about the first point); La Rocca 1997 (about the latter one).

[16] See, for example, Balzaretti 1996, pp.225-28.

[17] Ward Perkins 1983, p.124.

[18] See further chapter 2, in particular footnotes 72 and 77.

[19] Ciampoltrini-Notini 1990, p.590.

[20] Just in the 18th century, in fact, financial elements and market laws began to be deeply studied and understood (Ricardo); among previous times such courses or events seemed sometimes to be too distant to be correctly explained (to judge from the measures taken): clear examples could be the fall of the prices occurring in the Spanish Empire in about 1530-40 or inflation, which Medieval kings and states often tried to control by rising the nominal value of the currency (achieving exactly the opposite, because of the reduction of precious metal in the coins).

[21] See above note 13.

[22] As regards some towns from Calabria, for example, like Crotone or Reggio, it has been stressed on an interaction of them within an "international" trading network (but to what extent?) as late as the 8th and even the 9th century; Cuteri 1994, pp.341-42. On the other hand, in the Byzantine areas, the continuation of considerable exchanges until the 6th-7th century appears to have been due to strategic and political reasons; Christie 1990.

[23] Wickham 1994, pp.757-58.

come from the rise in productivity of the agricultural systems, beginning from the 8th-9th century (this being the only condition to produce enough surplus as to eventually invest in other activities too);[24] nevertheless, the geographical areas aforesaid (in particular Venice) have been often supposed to be fundamental as regards the social-economic changes of the very Early Middle Ages (Bognetti, Barnish, Hodges)[25] and this could mean, if not a "sliding", a tendency, at least, to turn interests also to other important centres: however it must be stressed these remarks can only show possible lines of research because of the lack of clear matches (especially archaeological and relevant to the early period),[26] even though a development in this sense would be hardly comparable with the merchant capitalism of the Late Middle Ages,[27] definitely directed towards the markets of Central and Northern Europe.

---

[24] Yet in the 10th century, the prosperity of Milan, for example, should have come from a strict relationship with its territory and production activities; Wickham 1999, p.4.

[25] See also Brogiolo-Gelichi 1998, p.43.

[26] Brogiolo-Gelichi 1998, p.159-60; Balzaretti 1996, p.219 and following.

[27] See also Wickham 1994, pp.752 and 757.

# 1. Economic aspects of the Early Medieval town

## 1.1. Fifth-seventh century town (pottery, production, commerce)

Several studies have in recent years regarded the economic elements of the town, particularly during the phases of transition from Late Antiquity, an essential starting-point to the best understanding of those more properly Early Medieval peculiarities.

The archaeological contribution is considerable and necessary, as literary sources are scanty and hardly "interested" in some aspects of material culture, moreover, although this kind of survey is obviously too limited, "the archaeological analysis of economy seems to be near a great deal" (Wickham 1994):[1] at least, as suggested by him, scholars have improved their interpretive patterns, accurately worked out in the light of the historical contexts and within problems as objectively as possible.

From the mid-5th century the existing political and economic orders were affected in a conclusive way by a succession of events, leading in turn to further events: without stressing a particular cause amongst them, the conquest of Africa by the Vandals, the fall of a strong, centralised system (the Roman one), the Greek-Gothic War as well as the coming of the Longobards, were all factors that, acting in that "long Late Antiquity" (5th-7th century), led the Italian peninsula from the Ancient to the Early Medieval world.

The reconstruction of urbanism is actually expected to take into account the diverse extent to which the regions concerned were hit by such events and, in the economic respect, the differences due to the various political roles (presence of the ruling classes and its actions), to the diverse strategic-military importance and to the new relationship between town and territory (it is often hard to distinguish what specifically lies within either of the two competences).

As regards material records, it must be stressed that pottery doubtlessly represents a primary guide for outlining trade as well as everyday life, but its prevalence could be mostly a result of its indestructibility, unlike other more perishable elements, which might have been largely used at the same time (whether for transport or cooking- and tableware).[2]

Nevertheless, having played a main role in production and trade throughout the whole Roman Age, this kind of study is certainly essential to point out those changes which affected the regions of the peninsula, once the influx of goods from overseas was curtailed and finally stopped (fig.1a, b): the distribution of Roman Red Slip Ware, its connection with workshops and local imitations show a "scrappy" view, beyond a general division into two main opposing blocs, one under Byzantine control and the other those regions conquered by the Longobards since 568.

The striking difference, though within the same administrative context, between the "vitality" of certain coastal towns or of considerable liaison centres and the ongoing degradation of some inland territories clearly marks an economic downturn, which the policy of Constantinople could only check in part, even if strictly concerning important institutional sites and due to diverse situations.

At the same time, a various series of solutions can be observed, ranging from a kind of continuity of the ancient technical background, especially where the trend of imported ornaments and commodities had become more deep-rooted, to the return of a prehistoric manufacturing, pigeon-holed for centuries, which emerged again where the "exotic taste" had less affected local traditions.

In Northern Italy, in the Po Valley regions, African Red Slip Ware was brought in quite late and African importations increasingly spread out up to the late 4th/first half of the 5th century: the circulation of types definitely standardized certainly influenced taste as well as local handicraft, which put its products on sale probably at a lower price, supplementing therefore the market of the original ones from Africa.

Imitations became diffused beginning from the late 4th century and they could be seen in the light of a great variety of productions that indicates several workshops within a territory-limited distribution network each.[3]

---

[1] *Considerazioni conclusive*, in Francovich-Noyé 1994, p.741.

[2] The changing of raw material is certainly plausible by the centuries of the Transition Age: Arthur rightly observes that the containers might have been of wood and so the knowledge of the range of commerce could be distorted for some areas; few finds have been reported by

Catarsi as regards *Fidenza* (nonetheless it is not sure they were relevant to the 7th-8th century layers of the concerned excavation); besides, late written sources (12th century) attest to the presence of *scodellari* in *Piedmont* (wooden-bowl manufacturers) and seem to describe a situation that had taken place previously. In spite of this, clear evidence is still lacking by the 7th century, in particular of any individual wooden vessel (*i.e.*, dish). Brogiolo-Gelichi, *La Ceramica comune in Italia settentrionale tra IV e VII secolo*, in Sagui 1998, p.143.

[3] Fontana, in Sagui 1998, p.54: it is difficult to detect the centres of manufacturing and their area of distribution, often hindered by the small number of kilns found by archaeology, especially in North Italy.

The archaeological matches attest ceramic typologies such as the so-called "*sigillata chiara padana*" (Po-Valley Light Red Slip Ware, widespread over the whole Lombard area from the 3rd to the 5th century) and also glazed pottery, characteristic of the inland zones throughout the 5th-6th century, which well deserves to be considered as replacing the imported articles, thus balancing, at the same time as other local productions, the remarkable drop in freight from overseas.

Such commodities did continue to reach those places, especially by the ports of *Aquileia* and *Ravenna*, through that river and lake network, the importance of which is particularly stressed as to the period between the mid-5th and the third quarter of the 6th century (Tortorella);[4] nevertheless, finds clearly show that by the mid-6th century, such a traffic involved only the main cities (and some strategic sites), where, however, the small percentages mark them to be of social rather than an economic importance.[5]

In Central and Southern Italy, and generally in those regions under the Byzantine influence, this pattern appears less quickly, but started just the same: considerable maritime exchanges still got to the towns, nonetheless, they were directed to those centres which were the seat of some administrative authority, this indicating that merchandise travelled over those routes kept up chiefly for military purposes (Panella).[6]

A great number of imports was eventually a good incentive to the local craftsmen, particularly in those urban sites which, due to their favourable geographical position, were able to play a role as key markets over a certain territory: the achievement of "Red Slip Ware" in Tuscany and *Emilia* can be given as a clear example, as well as several other fine products whose value was derived from classical standards and technologies, these

originating as new typologies to be considered as the basis for the Early Medieval manufactures.[7]

In spite of it, the suspension of tribute-payments by the Provinces, managed through the sound Roman distribution system, affected in a conclusive way the situation that was developing: in Tuscany, during the 6th century, a certain set of docklands was already in progress, mostly driven by the necessity for the Byzantines to keep themselves supplied and stay connected (the African commodities seem to have assembled only between *Vada* and *Cosa*: in the North just *Luni* shows some influx, that was not extended to its territory, whilst *Pisa* probably suffered a hard degradation, owing to the Greek-Gothic War);[8] in the inland areas of the *Piceno* region imports began to be reduced as early as the mid-5th century, and in the next century finds reflect desolate situations in this sense (just at the centre of *Suasa* some shards have been recorded); finally *Modena* and its surroundings is an interesting case, where an early isolation also seems to have affected its production, this becoming very characteristic over most of the peninsula, especially the northern part, throughout the central centuries of the Early Middle Ages.[9]

Because of the tendency towards less standardised manufactures and to a restriction of the territory concerned by their activity, research is expected to investigate thoroughly the diverse local typologies of ceramics as well as the range of their diffusion: after a study of the kind, it would be eventually possible to grasp all the technical and functional changes that occurred during Late Antiquity, also relevant to the economic situation and to the different dietary habits of the population, both in urban and rural contexts.[10]

Moreover, it is definitely fundamental to point out the extent and the way Roman tradition was still kept after

---

[4] Tortorella, in Saguì 1998, p.27. It is noteworthy that urban or fortified sites placed upon those waterways had always drawn a particular political attention, throughout both Late Antiquity and Early Middle Ages, insomuch that had they generally held specific administrative roles; furthermore, it can be mentioned that they were also important for the trading of soapstone, which required water transport because of its heaviness.

[5] Brogiolo-Gelichi, *Conclusioni*, in Brogiolo-Gelichi 1996, p.212. At Longobard-Age *Brescia* (as concerns the period until 650) the amount of the imported Red Slip Ware (far below 1% amongst the whole pottery finds) is extremely scant, nonetheless it has a cultural significance: still at that time, in fact, a part, though very limited, of the community demanded tableware of Late-Roman tradition.

[6] *Note conclusive*, in Saguì 1998, p.500: let us think also of fortified sites like *St.Antonino di Perti*, where imports even seem to have increased during the most dramatic pressure of the Longobard conquest; *Otranto*, fundamental Byzantine stronghold within the control network of the *Adriatic* Sea until the coming of the Normans in the 11th century, maintained several contacts with the Aegean areas (shown also by the persistence of manufactures which appear to be quite similar to the typologies found in the Oriental contexts). Staffa too (*Le produzioni ceramiche in Abruzzo tra fine V e VII secolo*, in Brogiolo-Gelichi 1996, p.198) has observed the same tendency among the main coastal centres of the *Abruzzi* region, at least until the mid-7th century.

[7] Staffa (see above note 6, p.198) reports the presence, at some important sites (*Pescara*, *Crecchio*), of locally-manufactured items close to specimens of eastern Mediterranean origin, definitely a hint of to the extent craftsmanship was affected, among those people, by the trendy adornments and techniques of the imported articles (which continued, at the same time, to reach those regions).

[8] Citter, *Trasformazioni della rete portuale e del regime di scambi lungo le coste della Toscana tra V e X secolo*, in Brogiolo 1996, pp.134-35. Tortorella (in Saguì 1998, p.27) points out that, as regards the period between the middle of the 5th and the third quarter of the 6th century, only from *Volterra* and *Pistoriae* come African Red Slip Ware sherds of some consequence.

[9] To judge from the famous "storing wells", it can be assumed that *Modena* and its territory were out of the main exchange networks of the *Emilia-Romagna* Region as early as the 6th century; specifically, the lack of the "*Classe*-type" ceramics is particularly significant. *Conclusioni*, in Brogiolo-Gelichi 1996, p.213; about "*Classe*-type" pottery, see Gelichi, in Saguì 1998; for *Suasa* and *Piceno*, Tortorella, in Saguì 1998, p.27.

[10] The success of simple bowls imitating Hayes 61b-type (as early as the end of the 4th-5th century), also suitable for containing semi-liquid food (*puls*), throws some light on the different dietary habits as well as on the means especially of the less well-to-do classes (Fontana, in Saguì 1998, pp.52-53).

the coming, at the end of the 6th century, of a new culture, the Longobard one, starting then to interact in some regions.

Nevertheless, the reconstruction of the town's economic system is as much complicated as it is incomplete.

Except for really few examples, there are no finds of any workshop or kiln that indicate the places where articles were originally manufactured: it is not possible, therefore, to draw a clear map of the main production-centres, nor the range of their territorial distribution; in short, current knowledge lacks a sufficient amount of material structures to define exhaustively Late Antique and Early Medieval towns as the former Roman.

Moreover, a comparison with the latter should be basic to understanding in depth any change happening or in the course of development.

The urban centres of the later Roman Empire emerge fairly defined as to their borders, with the artisan-quarters settled in the immediate suburbs or outside the city-walls (as well as the burial grounds), due to a certain *decorum*, to health regulations and abiding by the laws in force:[11] hence it means a great caring for the city, rather considered as administrative and consumption centre.

On the contrary, for the centuries we are here concerned about, there is even a great uncertainty whether to relate production structures to urban areas or not, and even in specific zones it is, nonetheless, difficult to quantify the available data as regards the economic strength of the centres and of their population; furthermore, it is hard to establish what ensued after the dismantlement of Roman buildings, if and what kind of planning or organization took place, making it even harder to achieve a clear and general interpretation: the results are rarely homogeneous and the analysis must be expected to start from very local contexts.

From the excavations, especially urban, concerning the early Lombard phases (end of 6th-first half of the 7th century) the picture that comes out shows characteristics as of radical change as of the kind of continuity, yet maintaining traditions and habits from the previous period.

By the coming of foreign groups of craftsmen some new centres sprang up, which eventually began to supplement the production of the extant workshops; new forms and techniques, in particular decoration, were then brought in, but also the large local background was actually still in use at the same time: indeed, contemporary with the typical Longobard pottery, commodities clearly deriving from Roman tradition were still manufactured, whilst

many items show an interaction with either cultural school.

Also the ways of settlement of artisan-shops did not cause a real upset to previous urban planning, on the contrary, they seem to have followed a process already in action for two centuries.[12]

At *Brescia* (fig. 2), handicraft activities appear as to have been installed just upon the west *portico* of the *Capitolium* (*Pallaveri* House),[13] a structure of which, perhaps for crockery-firing, has been dated to 592 AD (±160 years) by thermoluminescence: the occupation of areas spoiled or fallen in part into disuse has been already noted even on more ancient contexts (in Florence, upon the structures of the baths found under the present *Piazza della Signoria*, remains of a kiln related to glassworks were discovered and their dating indicates a range of time between the end of the 4th and throughout the whole 5th century at least).[14]

Beyond the west *portico* of the *Capitolium* some dwelling-places were excavated and they have been supposed to belong to artisans: the site (with post-holes for wooden structures and hearths) points out a humble context to be connected with the known servile class of people, whose activities included pottery-manufacturing, bone and metal-working, cattle breeding and cultivation, strictly subordinate to the court.

As regards the latter point, whereas the use of high quality Lombardic pottery could be due to the fact that there was a production of the kind, imported Red Slip Ware finds would be otherwise explained by the eventual presence of royal officials' residences nearby:[15] the area north of the *decumanus*, between the *Capitolium* and *St. Giulia*, should be considered, in fact, according to Brogiolo, as belonging to the royal court's lands.

Previously, Von Hessen also thought of *Brescia* as one of the main manufacture centres for the typical stamped and *stralucido* (a kind of glazed) pottery, characterized by

---

[11] See the example of *Altino*, where remains of Roman-Age kilns have been recently found; Cipriano – Sandrini, *Fornaci e produzioni fittili ad Altino*, in Brogiolo – Olcese 2000.

[12] The idea of a fierce conquest that had upset the order of Roman society emerges from the literary sources of the time (especially Byzantine, Brogiolo – Gelichi 1998, p.159): it had been followed by scholars until few decades ago, when new interpretations have begun to outline a milder picture, echoed by the archaeological results. Whilst the situation drawn by Bognetti (*S. Maria foris portas di Castelseprio e la Storia religiosa dei Longobardi*, in *L'età dei Longobardi* II, 1966, pp.141-52) stressed, in fact, a territorial planning mostly based on military strategy under the Longobards, Tabacco (recently, *Egemonie sociali e strutture del potere nel medioevo italiano*, 1992, p.119) has pointed out that local traditions and culture were at the same time to be found among the Germanic classes.

[13] Guglielmetti, *La ceramica comune fra fine VI e X secolo a Brescia, nei siti di casa Pallaveri, palazzo Martinengo Cesaresco e piazza Labus*, in Brogiolo – Gelichi 1996, p.9.

[14] Examples from several towns (*Verona*, Milan, *etc.*); for Florence see De Marinis-Pallecchi, in Mendera 1991, pp.27-28.

[15] Brogiolo and Guglielmetti (see note 13) think it probable, although any structures in this sense have not ever been found.

very fine mixtures, which seem to indicate a clay supply as from the same quarrying field.

Also samples from other cities (Milan, *Mantua*) show a certain similarity as to the technique or the mixtures and, once petrographic analyses confirmed it, an interregional trading of articles made in *Brescia* could be asserted.[16]

At this point it the places whereat those objects were found should be considered: before 1980, such evidence came solely from burial areas, some ritual function was therefore ascribed to the Longobard ceramics (in particular to the typical "drinking" wares).

Differently, in more recent excavations (besides *Brescia*, also at *Verona* in *Piazza del Tribunale*),[17] stamped and *stralucido*-decorated pottery was found in household contexts too, as kitchen- or tableware, even though with less niceties in the finishing-off.

Nevertheless, the most remarkable evidence comes from places of a certain political or strategic importance, wherein military or civil authorities might have established their residences aiming at the most effective control of the town: those very areas, indeed, which were public treasury properties, directly managed by the royal power through its officials;[18] moreover, the absence or the scant amount of Longobard pottery from any urban sites which were less important in a strategic respect, although related to contemporary phases should be stressed.[19]

This would support the idea of a kind of production and trading within a limited circulation, not ruled by free-market laws, but concerning the relationships within those lands owned either by the Court or by the Treasury.

Unfortunately, there are no excavations that have surely brought to light any site connected with urban power, more specifically any administrative or political centre to be eventually connected to the ruling classes: this would otherwise represent an essential contribution to the understanding of a possible relationship between the latter and a certain "elitist" production and circulation of commodities, a fact which would be fundamental to the

focus on the real economic strength of towns and the extent their population were engaged to.

However that may be, there is no doubt that, in Northern Italy, by the mid-7th century, not only pottery seems to be out of the international trading, but its production had also sharply declined, since either the Longobard or the Late Roman manufacture did not survive as late as that time, nor was any heritage handed down to the later manufactures.[20]

Over the central centuries of the Early Middle Ages, in fact, poorer standards took over, a reduction occurred to the number of typologies and, as a consequence, each piece could have more than one function: the so-called lidded-basin, a kind of stove (for bread baking) directly put upon the hearth-fire, is a clear example of the re-emergence of manufactures and habits which had been as characteristic of prehistoric times, but forgotten during the Roman era.

A decline in this sense can be noted in the fringe-zones as early as the 6th century, but it was striking and definitely widespread at the end of the 7th century: this certainly indicates social and economic as well as cultural changes, that marked the move "from bakery to portable stoves; from individual to collective cutlery; from collective to familiar provision" (Brogiolo-Gelichi).[21]

Finds show deterioration in coarse ware types generally all over the peninsula, regional comparisons were also progressively reduced, becoming possible only within very limited areas (remarkable examples are the provinces of *Padua-Treviso* and several sites along the Venetian coast).[22]

The most important cities, which were seats of some civil or religious authority, were also struck by the same occurrences, though to a different extent, and even in Rome, data from the *Crypta Balbi*[23] (that might have been hardly expected or imagined before) cannot be extended to the entire city. Moreover, it should be emphasised that certain dynamic exchanges often concerned luxury goods trading, which were usually connected to particular situations and classes, not really having a major effect on the economy of the society as a whole.

---

[16] Von Hessen's idea (1977) seems to be supported by recent excavation data too: besides Milan (*Piazza Duomo*), some shards of the kind come from *Mantua*, from a hut near the baptistery; on the other hand, at *Bergamo* certain finds would indicate local manufacture; (quoted by Guglielmetti, see note 13, p.6 and following).

[17] Hudson, *La dinamica dell'insediamento urbano nell'area del cortile del Tribunale di Verona*, "Archeologia Medievale" XII, 1985, pp.281-302.

[18] Examples in *Turin* (*Palazzo Madama*), at *Pavia* (see Hudson 1981), in Milan (near *Maximian*'s Walls), at *Brescia* (*domus* close to *St. Giulia*). De Marchi, *Modelli insediativi "militarizzati" d'età longobarda in Lombardia*, in Brogiolo 1995, p.39.

[19] Such a marked difference is evident not only among assemblages of pottery coming from excavations of districts which could be considered as socially similar, but also relevant to diverse quarters within the same town: whilst 800 pot-shards have been found at *St. Giulia*, in fact, other areas of *Brescia* are dramatically poor in this sense. See note 5.

[20] See note 5.

[21] *La ceramica comune in Italia settentrionale tra IV e VII secolo*, in Saguì 1998, p.148.

[22] See above note 5: coarse ware from the North-East of the peninsula can be compared until the 7th-8th century with typologies from *Istria* or *Slovenia*; on the other hand, by the 8th (Venetian region) and 9th century (provinces of *Padua* and *Treviso*) manufactures seem to be properly referred to a limited local scope. Concerning this, also the isolation of *Modena* can be remembered (*cf.* note 9 and Gelichi, *Ceramiche tipo "Classe"*, in Saguì 1998, p. 290-93).

[23] Ricci, in Paroli 1997; Saguì, in Saguì 1998.

Finally, by the second half of the 7th century, locally-made coarseware represented by far the most common manufacture and even in a mid- and long-distance commerce centre like Milan high percentages of them can be easily noticed, whereas the only glazed pottery (as well as soap stone) hardly seems to have balanced them.[24]

## 1.2. Town recovery

An interesting point is that such a kind of decline characterised, in particular, those geographical and chronological contexts, which are usually regarded amongst current interpretations as first steps of urban "rebirth".

It could then be agreed with Wickham's supposition that pottery is not a clear indicator of the economic system of the Early Middle Ages:[25] certainly, the 8th-9th century renewal, largely stated and accepted by scholars, was not really marked in northern Italy at least, by any valuable manufacture, whilst it is definitely reflected in other sectors like construction and notably emerging in the literary sources (over some regions north of River *Po*, for instance, fine pottery reappeared as late as the city-states' time, but architecture and documents do not leave any doubt about their considerable growth before this).[26]

In central and southern Italy, on the contrary, the so-called "*Forum Ware*" (thick-glaze-coated pottery, usually green)[27] became quite common, which could throw a certain light on the degree of development of some sites, insomuch that it well deserves to be considered a guide artefact from the 8th century onwards. Nonetheless, it is the first great manufacture that is properly Early Medieval: as a result, on the basis of technique and decorative specimens, as diverse as peculiar to different centres, it is sometimes possible to realize the "ups and downs" of a town during a certain period (for example, Naples seems to have reduced in part its production by the end of the 8th century because of the rise of *Salerno* and its port *Amalfi*).[28]

Nevertheless, either the lack or shortage of it over the central and northern regions of the peninsula cannot

actually indicate that "prosperity explosion"[29] of those areas (Barnish), which Bognetti had also paid a great attention to as lands marked by a considerable growth and changes throughout the 8th-9th century.

What research should then care about is doubtless the grounds of such an urban development and the ensuing reorganization of the territory, with which the towns seem to have become connected by a strong link: archaeology has therefore an important task and could play an essential role as to check this, also considering the availability of more numerous literary sources for that time.

Particularly regarding this point, written documents talk about the enormous riches hoarded up by means of thriving trade (as in the case of the doge *Partecipatio*); about the allotment of those state lands, which had remained frozen within kings' or dukes' properties throughout the first Lombard age, among the new main characters of *Po*-Valley economic system (bishoprics, monasteries, great lay landowners), nonetheless, the consequent management reorganization by the *curtis*, finally aimed also at purposes and interests more expressly urban.

So, these should be the main causes or, at least, a sort of "catalyst" and archaeology can well contribute to establishing the level at which agriculture, production and trade yielded the necessary resources for the renewed planning.[30]

Trade is often asserted as a decisive factor for the growth of towns especially by medievalists, who actually know very well the importance of this in the later city-state period; nevertheless, as regards the Early Middle Ages, a strict relationship between urbanization and commercial prosperity cannot be always taken for granted, as urban and merchant capitalism was not a definite term in the 8th century dictionary:[31] a clear example is *Rieti* that, although it held on to a certain institutional importance from the end of the 7th throughout the 8th century as the seat of the *gastaldus* (chamberlain), otherwise had an almost exclusively rural economy.[32]

The lines of communication still continued to work, land-roads still connected the Alpine passes with the *Po*-Valley regions and water-routes kept up a net composed of the River *Po* and its tributaries, which could cover most of North Italy by long-distance travelling as well as by cabotage or coasting. Archaeology has brought to light, in particular, the vast distribution of soapstone, which, according to some interpretations, was conveyed

---

[24] Excavation data from *Piazza Duomo* indicate a drop in coarseware from 73.5% (Late-Antiquity layers) into 58.1% (Early Medieval phases), but soapstone goes up that 15%, while glazed pottery is still at 20% odd. In many places coarseware reaches 80% (for instance, at *Sirmione, Lomello, Monte Barro*). A. Alberti, in Gelichi (ed.), *Atti del I Congresso Nazionale di Archeologia Medioevale*, 1997, p.338.
[25] Wickham (1981) asserts it again in *Early medieval archaeology in Italy: the last twenty years*, "Archeologia medievale", XXVI, 1999, p.9.
[26] Brogiolo-Gelichi 1998, p.41: fine examples are *St. Maria in Valle* at *Cividale, St. Salvatore* at *Brescia, St Maria foris portas* at *Castelseprio*.
[27] Ward Perkins, 1983, p.120; Brogiolo-Gelichi 1998, p.41.
[28] Paroli, in Brogiolo 1996, p.125, where the author emphasises the relationship between great commerce and circulation of glazed pottery (especially in the light of the cases of Rome and *Salerno-Amalfi*).

[29] Barnish, *The transformation of classical cities and the Pirenne debate*, "Journal of Roman Archaeology", 1989, pp.385-400.
[30] Brogiolo-Gelichi 1998, p.42.
[31] Wickham, *Conclusioni*, in Francovich-Noyé 1994, p.752.
[32] Arthur, in Francovich-Noyé 1994, p.429, where the difference between "successful and unsuccessful towns" is clearly stressed.

along the River *Rhone* to reach the *Ligurian* area, where it could be distributed for the central and southern regions of the peninsula up to the *Adriatic* coast[33] (fig. 3).

Important centres for warehousing and trading were those lake- and river-sites that maintained throughout Longobard and Carolingian times those characteristics which they held before from as early as the periods of the later Roman Empire and Late Antiquity (the former autonomous administrative units, the latter public treasury properties).[34]

Despite this, further research should be able to check the scope and real amounts of eventual business and, accordingly, establish the consequent bearings on the economic systems of town and country: it has often been the case that analysis has been based on too limited a number of finds that, far from representing exact economical indicators, only indicate obvious and "undeniable administrative, political or religious relationships between city.. and territory",[35] as well as between higher status families, over both short and long distances.

There is no evidence directly relating to any *emporia*, either on the Adriatic coasts or along the banks of the *Po*; what is more, towns such as *Aquileia* and *Ravenna* do not seem to have acted as redistribution markets for the region as a whole, but just for their immediate vicinity: there are no clear indicators, therefore, that can lead to a direct comparison of the Italian situation with northern European contexts, since even the so-called Type A *Emporia* (seasonal markets) [Hodges] appear not to have been represented across the northern districts of the peninsula.[36]

Hodges has put forward the hypothesis that *Charlemagne* did not try to conquer Venice (something he could have done without any particular difficulty) so as to protect the *trait d'union* between Venice, the Carolingian Kingdom and the Byzantine world: central-northern Italy was actually a key area and very much the heart of changes occurring in the 8th and 9th centuries, but unfortunately

there is no striking evidence of its actual economic capacity. What does raise questions about any considerable level of trade between the East and the *Po* Valley region is, ultimately, what could have been the corresponding exchanges for the exotic commodities, as soapstone alone seems hardly adequate to balance the imports of precious spices and fabrics.[37]

Also the famous *Liutprand Capitulary* (first half of the 8th century),[38] which has often been produced as a clear example, cannot really support the assumption of dynamic levels of exchanges: indeed, it might even be judged as an indicator of lower activity: salt, the product mentioned in the text, the carriage of which is conceded, is a necessity for daily life; moreover, the stated tolls to be levied at different centres are relatively low, almost "symbolic", as if indicating small volumes of freight traffic.

In addition, those towns, which appear from the document to be ports where *milites comaclenses* ships could berth, have not provided any convincing archaeological evidence: at *Mantua*, for example, there are only a few finds of Longobard pottery; at *Parma* and its environs (whereas, judging by that document, oil, corn and even pepper were demanded as tolls), surveys have pointed out a Longobard presence that was chiefly military (Gelichi 1989). Moreover, it cannot be deduced what the real economic weight exerted by the occupiers on local agriculture was on the sole basis of the cemeteries.[39]

Recent studies are more inclined to consider the various trades as quite limited exchanges within the scope and control of the state instead, aimed especially at providing luxury goods to meet the demand of those upper classes close to the Court.

According to this, the importance of certain sites should be seen rather in the light of their geographical and strategic position, irrespective of the settlement patterns as well as the territorial control imposed by the Longobard powers (putting back into perspective,

---

[33] Alberti, in Gelichi (ed.), Atti del I Congresso Nazionale di Archeologia Medioevale, 1997, p.337: the author reports finds on the River *Rhone*, where certain remains may support a form of trading in this sense. Staffa (in Sagui 1998, p.437 and foll.) remarks on the presence of soapstone at some sites of the *Abruzzi* region (*Pescara*).

[34] De Marchi (in Brogiolo 1995, p.35) notes that even *Cassiodorus* attests to the maintenance, still in the very early Longobard epoch, of a specific and particular juridical *status* for ports and centres upon watercourses.

[35] Brogiolo – Gelichi 1998, pp.157-58; Wickham also reasserts it (1999, p.1).

[36] Hodges in Christie – Loseby 1996, p.294.

[37] In agreement with Hodges, also Whitehouse, Carandini and Brogiolo – Gelichi (1998, p.43 and 160), who follow, on the basis too of new evidence, the old idea put forward by Bognetti (1948), asserting the importance of central-northern Italy in terms of the relations between the Carolingian Kingdom and the Papal State (in contrast with the shift of any political and economical centrality towards the regions upon the *Rhone* supported by Pirenne).

[37] In agreement with Hodges, also Whitehouse, Carandini and Brogiolo – Gelichi (1998, p.43 and 160), who follow, on the basis too of new evidence, the old idea put forward by Bognetti (1948), asserting the importance of central-northern Italy in terms of the relations between the Carolingian Kingdom and the Papal State (in contrast with the shift of any political and economical centrality towards the regions upon the *Rhone* supported by Pirenne).

[38] Mor (1977) dates it back to the first half of the 7th century, while scholars usually agree on the years 715-30 (Balzaretti, in Christie – Loseby 1996, p.219). This manuscript concerns the royal grant of trade rights (above all salt) along the River *Po*, specifically between (Byzantine) *Comacchio* and several ports of the *Po* Valley region.

[39] Most of those towns are scarcely known in an archaeological respect. Gelichi, during excavations at *Collecchio* (south-west of *Parma*) and *Castellarano* (south of *Reggio Emilia*), has only found large burial areas. According also to the results of Catarsi Dall'Aglio and Raggio (1993), he thinks that the Longobard impact on the territory must not have been of big consequence. Data reported by Balzaretti too, in Christie – Loseby 1996, pp.221-22.

however, Bognetti's interpretation, stressing too highly the militarised position).

Actually, as early as the first phase of the conquest, a new allocation of land and a different setting of the political functions of some centres were carried out: *Oderzo* was split up after being taken by *Grimoald* and its jurisdiction was shared out between the provinces of *Treviso*, *Ceneda* and *Cividale*. Certain places were raised to almost town status for different reasons but always within a policy of strengthening and consolidation pursued by the new rulers: *Sirmione*, *Pombia* and *Castelseprio* had institutional functions that may be called urban, taking the place of nearby Roman *municipia* (towns), which had remained under *Byzantium* (such as *Como*, and *Mantua* up to 603), with the intention of breaking off and balancing an extant territorial continuity related to the administration of Roman tradition.[40]

Concerning the 8th century (but possibly also earlier times too), the literary records tell of a class of *viri magnifici*, of *gasindi*, actually of *fidelites* (liegemen), who were granted landownership rights by the king, with the purpose of preventing the rise of strong, opposing centres (to be seen especially in the light of the internecine wars of the second half of the 7th century); in the same way should be considered any public treasury property (therefore subject to the crown) inside ducal lands or towns: the occupation and control of boundary areas as well as of strategic (close to the main gates, for instance, watching over the principal communication routes) and urban production quarters, were an essential responsibility of the Longobard authority, as is well reflected at several diverse sites, i.e. the *domus* of *St. Giulia* at *Brescia*, the zone near the *circus* at *Pavia* and that near the city walls of *Maximian* in Milan.

This could well support a certain disposition of the Longobard ruling classes to dwell within towns, but it also raises some questions about whether this had ever represented a spur to urban economic dynamism and whether (and to what extent) production followed free-market laws (then concerning the whole population, not just above-mentioned "elitist circulation"), or were connected with the military-supply needs, as the public treasury areas were often used for the quartering and manoeuvres of troops (especially at the time of the aforesaid civil strife, throughout the second half of the 7th century).[41]

Evidence from *Brescia*, *Cividale*, *Monza*, etc. show that only kings and great dukes (as well as bishops and important ecclesiastical institutions) could eventually afford to take over considerable building or service works, whilst lower-ranked nobles and officials had

actually smaller financial means: the Lombard upper classes appear to have been more urban, but definitely poorer than the former Late-Antique, and even the contemporary Merovingian-Carolingian, aristocracy and this must have undoubtedly affected the economic system of towns as a whole.[42]

What is more, a kind of administrative and institutional role was also undertaken by those fortified sites such as *Sirmione*, *Monte Barro* and *Castelseprio*, about which architectural and archaeological surveys have pointed out a certain level of prosperity. Apart from the remarkable monuments, some evidence of possible local production (of good quality too)[43] can be stressed, as well as imports, even if these could hardly be attributed to the initiatives of the merchant classes operating within free-market trading conditions, as those centres had developed mostly for defensive reasons directed towards the control of their territory.

In conclusion, the militarization occurring in society (a process already starting as early as Late Antiquity) should be carefully considered: it brought about a sharp economic improvement of those strategically important sites.

At this point, comparison should be made with the Byzantine *Liguria* (under the Empire up to 641), where excavation data indicate a large volume of imports from different Mediterranean coasts towards those *castra*, such as *St. Antonino di Perti*, that kept watch over the *Maritima Italorum* (fig. 4).[44]

According to Christie, that region seems to have remained under the Eastern Empire not only as a result of a strong defensive line held by means of many *castra* and garrisons (all the more so in that any clear fortified frontier has never been detected), but also because of the active interlocking of diverse Byzantine areas with each other, within a commercial framework carefully maintained by Constantinople.[45]

---

[42] For some examples of building in this sense see note 26; Gasparri (1980), quoted by Brogiolo-Gelichi (1998, p.159), points out that lands and real estate owned by officials were dependent on *emphyteusis*, mostly granted by kings or dukes; Wickham (*Conclusioni*, in Francovich-Noyé 1994, pp.751-52) observes that the Longobard nobles were more inclined to live in town, but he remarks that they were definitely less rich than the Late-Antique, Merovingian or Carolingian aristocracy.

[43] It has been put forward that there were glassworks at *Castelseprio*: some faulty pieces (presumably rejects) were excavated; nevertheless the data do not seem to be enough to sustain such an assertion. Nepoti, in Mendera 1991, pp.117-18.

[44] Gardini-Murialdo, *La Liguria*, in Francovich-Noyé 1994, p.170. Confirmation of a kind has emerged too from the tireless work of Nino Lamboglia, as well as from the following studies of Tiziano Mannoni.

[45] Christie, *Byzantine Liguria: an imperial province...*, "Papers British School at Rome", 1990, pp.229-71, accepted by Gardini-Murialdo, in Francovich-Noyé 1994, p.170; Staffa (*La città altomedievale...*, in Gelichi [ed.], Atti del I Congresso Nazionale di Archeologia Medievale, 1997, p.71 and following) points out that, in the 6th and 7th centuries, the most important towns on the coasts of *Abruzzi* and *Molise* (*Pescara*, *Teramo*) also took part in the exchange network which connected the

---

[40] De Marchi, in Brogiolo 1995, p.43.

[41] De Marchi (in Brogiolo 1995, p.44) deals with this subject exhaustively; see this reference also for the sources about the *fideles* (p.39 and note 40).

As a result of this, once those sites and regions lost strategic importance, imports fell sharply, this pointing out that freight followed the same routes that were used mainly for military purposes.[46]

Despite this, the steep downturn in such trade should not be attributed exclusively to the Longobard conquest, but also to the lack of any local commercial organization of real consequence. In fact, if some mercantile activities did continue, they seem to have depended strictly on demand and on the assets of limited centres or groups of people. Therefore, far from being a generalised situation, the contexts often mark large differences in terms of pottery types and quality, as is well reflected archaeologically – for example in some records from Genoa compared to others found at *Luni* (where manufacturers appear to have been mostly local).[47]

As concerns the period between the 7th-8th and the 10th centuries, Paroli asserts the existence of a considerable trade in glazed pottery, globular *amphorae* and luxury goods, as well as other more common articles, which seem to have involved towns (but not exclusively) across southern and central Italy and northwards to the Tuscan and *Ligurian* coasts up to southern France, supporting the idea that a significant level of commercial dynamism never totally waned, and that this was particularly so in some contexts[48] (fig. 5a, b).

A few remarks should be but put forward at this stage.

First, a very fragmented situation can easily be noticed within the same regional areas. In *Liguria*, as mentioned above, differences emerged even between sites that were quite close to each other. Similar indications come from Tuscany where, if in the central and northern areas some Early Medieval glazed pottery has been found (of the 8th century at Pisa [*Piazza Dante*]), nevertheless, most exchanges must refer to a sub-regional circulation (Citter).[49] Concerning France, the data from here cannot be extended to the whole coastline, although certain

findings are remarkable (both archaeological and literary);[50] Finally, within the *Campania* region, the evidence shows the ups and downs in the commercial activities first of Naples, and then of *Salerno* and *Amalfi*.[51]

Research, therefore, should also exclude a generalised analysis, since the geographic and chronological starting points hardly seem to extend beyond a rather limited context, compared, for instance, to the great influx in ancient times of international commodities (over more or less the entire peninsula), which was consequent, however, on the tributes owed by the Roman provinces.

On the contrary, in terms of the centuries in question, the economic scope of each centre or region was very different, as were the causes and extent of its development. The intent of the Church was to maintain and foster important connections with its southern landed properties (such as the *Calabria* region – lost in about 730) and to assert its authority over the territory of *Latium* and *Campania*. In France, the wealthy Carolingian landowners were even able to foster a considerable trade in oriental items. Furthermore, considerable Roman traditions survived at times in certain areas of production, or exchanges, and were more deep-rooted within certain contexts.[52]

Rome itself, a far important market, and where the presence of merchants from Venice and *Amalfi*[53] is also well documented as early as the 8th century, seems to have depended on regional supply throughout the 7th and 8th centuries, whereas trade in items such as wine from

---

Adriatic regions with each other, northwards up to the fortified site of *Invillino*. Gasparri (in Brogiolo 1995, p.9 and following) firmly doubts that there was a continuous and well-defined borderline defended by Byzantine garrisons, reinforced during the advance of the Longobards. On the contrary, material finds from some sites of *Piedmont* would rather show contacts with the *Ligurian* context, so that a quite "open frontier" may be supposed.

[46] Panella, in Saguì 1998, p.500.

[47] Biagini – Melli – Torre, in Saguì 1998, p.351 and foll.: data are still preliminary as regards some quarters of the city (*Mattoni Rossi*; the area near *St. Lorenzo*'s Cathedral). A comparison seems to be likely with the district of *Invillino* (*Udine*), regarding the persistence of certain exchange items (as is also observed within the *Abruzzi* region [Staffa, in Saguì 1998, p.437 and foll.]).

[48] See Paroli, in Brogiolo 1996; for southern France (*Languedoc*) see the contribution of Pellecuer, in Brogiolo 1996, pp.126-32.

[49] In Brogiolo 1996, pp.133-37: here focus is on the salt trade in terms of its particular interest for the aristocracy of *Pisa* and *Lucca*: moreover, the author reconstructs the possible routes (also attested to by 8th-century sources). Once transported from the mines to the shores of *Maremma*, it may have been carried by coastal navigation, perhaps to *Pisa*, where it could eventually take the land route to *Lucca*.

[50] The results from *San Peyre* (see note 48 above) put firmly back in perspective the interregional contacts between France and the Mediterranean during the Early Middle Ages, illustrating the considerable means of the Frankish ruling classes, irrespective of their capacity to develop trade of consequence. Paroli (in Brogiolo 1996, p.123) mentions the case of the town of *Arles*, as described by a literary source of 798 ("*versus Theodulfi episcopi contra iudices*"), wherein the bishop disapproved of the behaviour of the local judges, who were bribed with items that were typical of Eastern countries. Some glazed shards from *Arles* have surfaced from 9th-century layers (to be ascribed probably as products of *Latium*).

[51] It is interesting to remember that Naples may plausibly have been a sort of "*emporium*" under the Longobard dukes from the 7th century, even if clear written evidence date just from the 9th century (Wickham, in Francovich – Noyé 1994, p.750); for *Salerno* and *Amalfi*, see *infra* note 28.

[52] In Naples, at *Capua* (Arthur – Patterson, in Francovich – Noyé 1994, p.414), as well as at *Pescara*, *Crecchio* and *Teramo* (Staffa, in Saguì 1998, pp.274 and foll., 284), some groups of ceramics show high-level technique, acquired by the local craftsmen during Late Antiquity and inherited by the Early Medieval manufactures. Pottery coated with a thick glaze found in *Abruzzi* may date back to the 6th century, a fact which would demonstrate its contemporaneousness (and thus a common technical background at least), with the artefacts imitating African or Oriental models. Staffa himself (*i.e.*, in Brogiolo – Gelichi 1996, p.203) remarks that certain decorations and techniques, which clearly drew inspiration from Eastern patterns, survived as late as the 10th-11th centuries (in particular at *Otranto* and in the centres within its sphere of action).

[53] Paroli mentions the *Liber Pontificalis*, in which is mentioned the important role of those merchants in the slave trade, notwithstanding an attempt to limit it (in Brogiolo 1996, p.124).

the south should rather be considered as luxury and occasional goods.[54]

In any case, the growth of commerce should be seen as a consequence, rather than a reason for the recovery of the towns, the eventual prosperity of which is usually thought to have come from the local economy, and in particular from robust agricultural systems within their territory, that was able to yield a surplus that could have subsequently helped develop other activities as well.[55]

The real question is whether the requisite conditions for sustainable production systems ever existed, and especially in those geographical areas that were apparently less stable as a result of foreign invasions or warfare generally.

Tabacco had already pointed out that, after the upset of the first phase of the Lombard conquest, a certain stability began to take progressive hold – a consequence of improved relations with local elements; of a trend towards Roman customs among some ranks; and with the result that some features of the German society, became later more susceptible to the influence of an advanced culture.[56]

Moreover, the arrival of the Carolingians did not throw the administrative institutions into any particular confusion, as in most cases Frankish officials were merely substituted for the former Longobard ones.

By that time, the (previously begun) practice was finally developed and consolidated whereby assets and rights could be transferred to religious bodies. This included, for example, monasteries, which seem to have had a decisive share in the general reorganization, as well as in the improvement of the relationship between town and territory.[57]

Brogiolo properly remarks that, as regards the *Po* Valley region, the recovery occurred even earlier than the foundation of most of the great urban monasteries. What is more, they 'inherited' ducal or fiscal lands with pre-existing levels of output, and after all, they represented only a part 'of the institutions… of the ecclesiastical apparatus which featured… the urban context'. It is well known that a leading role was played by bishops in the government of the Byzantine cities, in particular Rome, *Ravenna*, Naples, and that there may well have been similar Church influence for the Longobard towns, at least from the time of *Liutprand*.[58]

In addition, the survival of a large amount of documentary evidence from monasteries should also certainly be attributed to the fact that they themselves were one of the most effective means for the preservation of manuscripts.

Although these objections must surely be taken into account, nevertheless, some evidence, both written and archaeological,[59] seems to suggest that they had a definite role in the development of the economic system, beginning from the second half of the 8th century. Manuscripts from *St. Salvatore* at *Brescia* (dated from around 760) indicate a number of assets owned by that monastery within the town itself and the bordering territories (where they increased noticeably throughout the 9th century); furthermore, that monastery had a certain control over the port of *Piacenza*. For the year 862, the monastery of *St. Columba* at *Bobbio* is attested to have been granted properties, enabling rights and transit duties *in portu de Mantua* (Inventories, 138).[60] There is also evidence from *St. Ambrose* in Milan concerning several possessions dating from 835 (including the Church of St. John the Baptist at *Monza*, founded by *Theodolind*).

Since they were often situated within or close to a town, the monastic communities eventually represented an important link between rural and urban contexts: their activities concerned purchasing, selling, and generally

---

[54] Delogu, in Francovich – Noyé 1994, pp.10-11; Paroli – Delogu 1993, p.17.

[55] The most recent studies seem to support such a line of interpretation: among them Wickham (1981, 1994, lastly "Archeologia Medievale", XXVI, 1999, pp.9-15); Brogiolo – Gelichi 1998, p.160; Delogu (see above note 54).

[56] See *infra* note 12. The advance of the Longobards affected in a conclusive way especially those territories around the new borders; nonetheless the advance also had a bearing on the changes that had already taken place for two centuries (Gasparri, in Brogiolo 1995, pp.9-18). However fierce an invasion may be, the situation usually tended sooner or later towards a certain political stability, which was definitely a fundamental condition for steady and more prosperous economic systems: e.g. the central and southern Danube regions, where two states had originated from the raids of the Hungarians and the Bulgars (respectively at the end of the 9th and in the second half of the 7th century), which may also be also seen ultimately as a sort of defence against further attacks and consequent disruption.

[57] Balzaretti, in Christie – Loseby 1996, pp.225-28.

[58] Brogiolo – Gelichi 1998, p.160. The authors stress the small production output from certain monasteries had (except the most important ones); moreover, Cantino Wataghin (quoted by Balzaretti, in Christie – Loseby 1996, p.226) has demonstrated that some of their foundation dates should be postponed – specifically to a time when a certain level of urban recovery had already begun.

[58] Brogiolo – Gelichi 1998, p.160. The authors stress the small production output from certain monasteries (except the most important ones); moreover, Cantino Wataghin (quoted by Balzaretti, in Christie – Loseby 1996, p.226) has demonstrated that some of their foundation dates should be postponed – specifically to a time when a certain level of urban recovery had already begun.

[59] Excavation data from the *Crypta Balbi* and *St. Vincenzo al Volturno* suggest high-status productions and widespread exchanges, including items for Longobard consumers (Hodges, in Francovich – Noyé 1994, pp.112-16). Certain articles appear to show international contacts (in the Roman monastery, bone splinters from a species of Irish deer were found: an animal that became extinct on the Continent just after the last Ice Age [Ricci, in Paroli 1997, note 174]. This evidence is of interest, but admittedly it is too restricted in terms of its impact on the overall reconstruction of local economy and trade).

[60] Literary sources quoted by Balzaretti, in Christie – Loseby 1996, p.221 and 227.

undertaking exchanges that involved agricultural products as well as town markets.[61]

Moreover, they were usually linked to the aristocracy and to their economic interests; therefore it can be asserted that, like other ecclesiastical (bishoprics in particular)[62] or lay institutions, monasteries must have had a considerable part to play in the management and reorganization of those lands that had remained unexploited since the 7th century. These productive areas, once renewed and developed as part of well-managed and lasting economic systems, would have also been able to produce surpluses that would enable communities to also invest in other activities, including eventually long-distance trade (Wickham 1981).[63]

## 1.3. Final remarks.

Ceramics, especially from Africa, had been a main feature of Roman commerce (transport containers, store- and kitchen-ware), in both home and export 'markets', and often influenced by foreign types and styles.

The imports (and also the imitations, which show a certain trend), analysed on the basis of historical events, can shed light on the changes that affected both urban and rural economic systems during the period of transition (5th-7th centuries): changes that indicate several developments that ensued, among diverse contexts, after the fall of the centralised organization for the widespread distribution of commodities.

Different distribution marked the 'fringe zones', or the regions that were subdued in the Longobard conquest, or the areas subject to Byzantium, where the decline in imports was slower; a relatively stable influx of foreign merchandise however emerged only from those cities or fortified sites that seem to have been particularly important in a political, administrative or strategic sense.[64]

However, the historical reconstruction of the urban economy and of its framework is hindered by the shortage (or lack) of evidence, both literary[65] and archaeological, relating to some fundamental questions: for instance, regarding production, the possible replacement of raw material with perishable elements is only seen from very late sources,[66] whereas the few structures found from field surveys, such as kilns, do not illustrate any complete or definite pattern.[67]

It cannot be established, therefore, where production actually occurred (if specifically within the town boundaries) and, generally, if what followed after the dismantlement of the ancient production system was somehow influenced by monastic rule had had eventually become common practice.

It cannot thus be fully understood to what extent the post-Roman towns differed from the previous ones, nor whether they were already displaying characteristics that might be considered as anticipating the following (proper) medieval period, nor if and how they could ever match contemporaneous Eastern or Middle-Eastern models, where the Roman planning was likewise 'disrupted', and stores and workshops arose instead, featuring those markets (the *suq* and *bazaar*), so typical of Islamic cities.[68]

A striking factor was undoubtedly the militarization of society, as a result of new requirements, especially for defence. Such a process, already under way as early as

---

[61] Balzaretti (see *infra* note 57, pp.227-28) refers to 'dispensae' of monasteries, i.e. at Pavia, where the agricultural surplus was stored (unfortunately there is no clear archaeological evidence before the 10th century).

[62] The importance of the bishop is revealed by his role in urban administration and affairs (as indicated by the written sources, in particular relating to disputes between Episcopal churches and towns). Two examples are quoted from Balzaretti, in Christie – Loseby 1996, pp.221-22: the bishop of Parma (as a result of a charter of *Charlemagne* in 781) had the right to collect taxes for the Frankish Crown; and in 851-52, *Louis II* upheld the arguments of the bishop of *Cremona* (*Placita* 56) regarding the levying of tolls from the merchants of *Comacchio*.

[63] Wickham, 1981, pp.96-97.

[64] The 6th-7th century '*Samos* cistern type' *amphora* has only been found, for example, at the most important ports (Rome/*Porto*, Naples, *Ravenna/Classe*), and at minor sites that can be linked to the strategic interests of Byzantium (*castra* of north-eastern Italy, the territories of Naples and Sicily); Arthur – Patterson, in Francovich – Noyé 1994,

p.414. On the other hand, there is no evidence of such *amphorae* in *Liguria* (Paroli, in Brogiolo 1996, p.122). Nevertheless, exchanges even seem to have increased there during the periods characterised by a dramatic tension with the Longobards (to be seen also in the light of Christie's idea, *infra* note 45), whereas the presence of certain new transport containers (*amphora a fondo umbonato* ['boss-shaped base'], manufactured not earlier than the end of the 6th century) shows the persistence of extensive trade with important sites and strongholds, such as *St. Antonino di Perti*; Gardini – Murialdo, in Francovich – Noyé 1994, p.170.

[65] The uncertainty (or at least the lack of unanimity) among the literary sources themselves about the concept of city and its features makes the interpretation sometimes more difficult; for the Anonymous of *Ravenna* (IV, 36) *civitas* is any inhabited and agglomerated centre enclosed by defensive walls with specific institutional seats (either religious, civil or fiscal), clearly distinguished by *castrum* and *oppidum* mentioned by Paul the Deacon (De Marchi, in Brogiolo 1995, p.11); some *castra*, placed around certain towns, according to the so-called strategy of "defence-in-depth", seem to have rather been populated sites with military functions, where local people were also engaged for building and maintenance works (*Conclusioni*, in Brogiolo 1995, pp.239-40); besides, a confusion of terms (*castrum, castellum, urbs, civitas*) can be noticed even as regards centres of the same region but recalled by diverse authors (examples from the Upper-*Adige* [*Süd Tirol*] district; Dal Ri – Rizzi, in Brogiolo 1995, p.88).

[66] See *infra* note 2 about the 12th-century *scodellari* of *Piedmont*, who however may reflect an ordinary and older situation too. In any case, it is quite hard to establish the real weight of these artefacts on the economy and market.

[67] For example, kilns where imitations of African Red Slip Ware (*sigillata*) were manufactured have left poor remains and, what is more, they have been ascertained only in the central and southern regions of the peninsula (Fontana, in Saguì 1998, p.53).

[68] Wickham, in Francovich – Noyé 1994, p.747.

the 4th century, brought about a stricter state control of the administrative institutions, among which public officials and other magistrates (likewise elective posts) did survive up to the 6th century (also in Byzantine territories), but faded slowly into the background, being then substituted by such hierarchical functionaries as the *comes*, the duke, and the *tribunus*, who were invested with both civil and military authority.[69]

Yet in the 4th century, the existence of state factories in some towns (arrows at *Concordia*, armour at *Cremona*, swords at *Lucca*, as well as other manufacturing at *Venosa* and perhaps at *Reggio Calabria*; fig.6) should be proof of the aforesaid development, even in the sphere of production,[70] according to Whittaker, who has asserted that in Late Antiquity commerce was eventually managed and ruled by the State and large landowners, rather than by any free market.[71]

There is but little evidence to outline the organization of these centres from the later Roman Empire; moreover it is hard to establish any kind of connection or continuity with the Byzantine *ergasteria* or the Longobard court-workshops (the activity of which might even be considered, according to some hypotheses, as being intended for exclusive circulation within certain fiscal areas).[72]

Nevertheless, some points are quite clear: the Tetrarchic-Age town itself, which had recovered after the ups and downs of the 2nd century, seems to have been very different from that of Augustan times, since when not only its planning was transformed, but also the idea of the 'city' itself no longer reflected the classical standard of the first century AD,[73] whilst its development was marked by new strategic and military demands – something that also happened throughout the centuries of transition and the Early Middle Ages.

Between the 5th and the 7th centuries its relationship with the surrounding territory faded away or changed

radically.[74] Public resources, formerly destined for towns, were often allocated to fortified sites, especially in certain border zones,[75] for which scholars have recently indicated a very varied type of frontier, owing its forms and structures to the different junctures of each region: a kind of 'permeability' (in an economic sense), seems to have characterised, for instance, the defensive line of *Liguria*, while some commercial contacts eventually continued between the northern *Adriatic* ports and the *castrum* of *Invillino*[76] (fig. 7). On the contrary, within some contexts, there were striking differences between the Byzantine areas and those territories controlled by the Longobards during the second phase of the conquest, bringing about a significant change in both rural population and the socio-economic status of towns.[77]

An example comes from the situation south of Tuscany. As emerges from Lombard laws and administration, there was a strict control of that frontier,[78] the limits of which were established without considering the old urban boundaries, and sometimes blocking off the lines of communication. As a result, serious instability developed, to judge from the transfer of diocesan seats, and there was a reduction of contacts and decrease in exchanges: *Tarquinia*, already in decline, was strongly affected by the nearness to the frontier and so the bishop was transferred to *Tuscania* before the year 595.[79] *Agnellus Ravennatis* talks about few arrangements or changes occurring to the communication system of the Byzantine regions, but, on the other hand, what is told by Gregory the Great regarding the 'cruel conquest' of *Ferento* by the Longobards should support the fact that the boundary along the River *Mignone* was not exclusively a juridical barrier, but must also have been characterised by a severance of relations, as is clearly shown by the lack of any trading between the two opposing regions.[80]

In spite of a state of insecurity within some geographical contexts, it can be noticed, however, that even in regions that were greatly damaged, such as *Abruzzi* and *Molise*,

---

[69] Brogiolo – Gelichi 1998, p.157.

[70] *Ib.*, pp.156-57.

[71] Whittaker, *Trade and the Aristocracy in the Roman Empire*, 'Opus', 4, pp.49-75.

[72] Brogiolo – Gelichi 1998, p.157. 8th-century written sources (probably reflecting even more ancient situations) indicate a significant presence of craftsmen of Roman tradition (smiths, goldsmiths, coiners) in towns strictly connected with the Court or the elite classes (*Pavia*, Milan, *Monza*, *Lucca*, etc.). With regard to manufactures of shields and, in particular, shield bosses, the so-called '*Po* Valley' style, based on decoration typology, suggests that the *ateliers* were in Milan, at *Pavia*, at *Cremona*. Such locations would recall the weapons factories of Late Antiquity (arrows at *Concordia*, armour at *Cremona*, swords at *Lucca*, etc.) and, consequently, the same network of roads through which those items were delivered, over the regions of the kingdom from *Tuscia* up to the Canton of *Ticino*; De Marchi, in Brogiolo (ed.), Atti del II Congresso Nazionale di Archeologia Medievale, 2000, pp.284-86.

[73] *Considerazioni conclusive*, in Gelichi 1999, p.139.

[74] *Luni*, for example, an important Byzantine military site, did not really interact with its territory, since (imported) goods do not seem to have been traded outside the town (Citter, in Brogiolo 1996, p.13).

[75] *Giorgio Ciprio* mentions some *castra* from the *Abruzzi* region: specifically, the Byzantines must have fortified *Kàstron Nòbo* in order to hold (for a while) their position and control over part of the coast near *Teramo*, after *Castrum Truentinum* had been conquered by the Longobards (around 580); Staffa, in Brogiolo 1995, p.189 and note 25 for the reference to the source concerned.

[76] *Infra* note 45.

[77] Brogiolo – Gelichi 1998, p.157.

[78] Kurze – Citter, in Brogiolo 1995, p.169 and note 81 for the relevant sources on the administration of the sites upon the frontier.

[78] Kurze – Citter, in Brogiolo 1995, p.169 and note 81 for the relevant sources on the administration of the sites upon the frontier.

[79] *Ib.*, p.169.

[80] The large gap between the material data from Tuscany and *Crypta Balbi* would, if confirmed, be a clear indication in this sense. Moreover, after the fall of the frontier at the end of the 8th century, finds seem to reflect new contacts and commercial exchanges between southern Tuscany and the area of *Latium/Campania*; Citter, *ib.*, p.174. For the development of the Byzantine defensive system, *ib.*, pp.174-77.

after the harshness of the first period, communications slowly recovered and small volumes of exchanges seem to have resumed within a local or regional circulation (Staffa).[81]

These are not remarkable signs, but nonetheless they show a tendency towards a certain political and economic order, which is mostly evident in northern Italy, although generally slow and fluctuating in terms of duration and ways of development.

By the fall of the 7th, and throughout the 8th century, a conclusive factor was the appearance (or at least the stronger presence) of the ecclesiastical institutions as regards the management of the production system, contemporary with the organization of that carried out by the *curtis*.[82] The importance of the bishop emerges from several documents (often concerning disputes against towns) that clearly point out the considerable episcopal share in the economy of the cities and their surrounding territories (juridically attested also by imperial decrees or charters);[83] Nonetheless, other religious bodies, such as monasteries, although their chronological achievement (as well as the extent of it) is quite controversial, could well encourage improvements in the relationship between urban and rural contexts. Monasteries should not be underrated as they were firmly linked to the aristocracy (by which they were often founded and/or granted assets); moreover, they usually attended to the lands and interests of aristocratic families (both inside and outside the city walls), retaining this function even when their activities seem to have been more independent and autonomous.[84] In one way, it might be said that they supported the demilitarization of the economic sector, directing the production of the recovering agricultural systems towards more freely run markets.[85]

---

[81] As the frontier between Longobards and Byzantines was established and defined (around the 620-30s), a level of contact appears to have resumed. In the inland region of *Abruzzi*, the presence of painted (*a bande*) pottery (comparable, in part, with the 'Crecchio'-style decoration) draws a parallel with the situation that emerged from the well-known Longobard *necropolis* of *Castel Trosino*, where (imported) African lamps have been found; Staffa, in Brogiolo 1995, pp.227-28.

[82] *Infra*, text and note 30.

[83] See *infra*, note 62.

[84] Balzaretti, in Christie – Loseby 1996, p.226.

[85] See *infra*, note 61.

# 2. The material structures of the Early Medieval town

## 2.1. Boundary walls and new defensive and organizational systems.

City walls have for a long time attracted the attention and interest of scholars. This was often because of their 'imposing' presence, especially before stratigraphical excavations developed, and, as they are clearly defensive structures, they well symbolize warring times – as the Middle Ages have always been considered.

This iconic element of urban topography has been studied – in terms of its modification, repair, restoration – to improve our knowledge of towns and their post-classical phases. The boundaries of city walls (if reconstructed) have often been used to check the full extent of Early Medieval sites, and comparisons made between the latter plants and the respective Roman ones (theoretically easy to outline), in attempts to trace (sometimes too hurriedly) possible continuations (or not) in different urban contexts.[1]

The study of each case is definitely a good starting point in terms of understanding both the function and functioning of fortifications over the centuries. Nevertheless, material structures should be then considered within a wider scope, so that the field data can be analysed in the light of socio-political changes and historical events, which might have brought about, on a local or interregional base, different solutions and developments, with relation, in particular, to the diverse relationships between town and countryside.[2]

An important survey has recently been carried out, researching into the changes of Late Antique defence systems, which appear to have been based on a so-called 'strategy in depth'[3] rather than on any secure and well-defined *limes*. The results are incomplete, but the main outlines can be traced (with the aid of some notable literary sources, i.e. the *Notitia Dignitatum*, a document, dated to 425 and suggesting for the first time a military

organization concerning the Alpine regions (*tractus circa Alpes*). Under the authority of a *comes* and consisting only of several *castra* and fortified sites, it controlled the main roads as well as the access to important geographical areas (fig.7).

These *castella* were often developed by the state, but some of them existed before that time, built on the initiative of local communities[4] and, once readjusted to meet the new requirements, they could easily have the same role as the others.

Research (in particular regarding the Alps and Pre-Alps regions) has pointed out that the erection of those sites did not begin earlier than the end of the 4th century. This is of interest, as a 'castle defence' system[5] would have ensued after certain events which had affected the northern regions of the peninsula, such as the breeching of the Rhine *limes* by the Alemanns in 407 or the Gothic incursions.

Negro Ponzi well advises not to extend this 'model' generally across the whole of northern Italy, as would be easy to do, judging from the contemporaneous building of most of the sites concerned (especially in the eastern area of the *Po* Valley) and also from the analogies of the techniques employed there.[6] Settlement types, such as those situated on a prominence or hilltop (of whatever level of fortification), as well as rural villages spread throughout the plain near to rivers and important roads, already existed in Roman times, being part of a network aimed at controlling outposts or those territories that were too exposed. Some of those sites, moreover, did not have exclusively military functions, but seem to have been inhabited by local people who could also find protection inside them (as indicated by the presence of churches at *Castelseprio*, *Ragogna* and in the *Comacina* Island).[7]

In some contexts there is a chronological uncertainty in terms of any process of organization, so that other causes

---

[1] The city walls of *Piacenza*, for instance, although not exactly known, seem to have been rebuilt during the Late Antique epoch, following quite closely the previous circuit which dated to the period of Roman colonization (a fact perhaps due to the conformation of the ground rather than to a real stability of the centre). In addition, its urban planning results in one of the best preserved sites in the region of *Emilia*, matching perfectly with the present one. This should make scholars take note, because the literary sources describe it as the most rural town within the ancient *Regio VIII*. Brogiolo – Gelichi 1998, p.54 and 60.

[2] Brogiolo points out the importance of an accurate survey over the territory to understand 'the very varied development of each urban centre'. *Conclusioni*, in Brogiolo 1995, p.244..

[3] Gasparri, in Brogiolo 1995, p.9.

[4] *Introduzione*, in Brogiolo 1999, p.10.

[5] *Ib.*, p.11.

[6] Caution is required when a 'uniform model derived from official patterns' is put forward, as even sites belonging to the same district or context show at times several differences in respect of planning and building techniques; moreover, similar architectural solutions cannot be always considered explanatory as regards either the geographical or chronological range, since Justinian-era castles in North Africa match very closely the examples concerned here. Negro Ponzi, in Brogiolo 1999, pp.148-49.

[7] It is possible that many such sites developed into populated agglomerations and so lost their exclusive military function (still maintaining, however, the role of fortified centres). On the other hand, there are some contrasting cases, such as in the *Adige* Valley, where most sites appear to have been inhabited *nuclei* from the very beginning, or at *Ragogna* (*Reunia*), where the baptismal church is plausibly older than the fortification. *Introduzione*, in Brogiolo 1999, p.11.

may also be presumed, such as, for example, the early crisis and collapse that affected the towns of *Piedmont*, or the presence of settlement and housing patterns of prehistoric tradition that survived on the fringe of rural and urban planning throughout the earlier Roman Empire.

Nevertheless, even taking into account all these remarks above, a decisive change should be assumed regarding defence strategy, the new basis of which prove to have been typical not only of Late Antiquity, but, with some variances, they also characterised the Gothic Age as well both Byzantine and Longobard areas. On the other hand, the abandonment or, more exactly, the loss of 'military function' at some castle sites (especially in the Pre-Alpine regions) should thus be seen as a shift of the frontier, and the battlefront, rather than any change to that pattern.[8]

Towns were dramatically affected by these changes and their walls can actually represent an important indicator outlining the diverse planning of urban space, as well as to aid our understanding of the developing defensive and organizational policies evolved to meet the new historical course of events. In fact the Italian regions, at an early period in the North, were shaken, after a long-lasting peace,[9] at first by occasional raids (such as those in the mid-Adriatic area in the years 270-1), and then by more conclusive events that transformed the peninsula into a battlefield for several armies throughout the centuries of transition.[10]

The reconstruction of the boundary walls of *Rimini* is dated to the end of the 3rd century (to the time of *Aurelian*), whilst those at *Parma* (although the excavation data are scanty), although probably contemporary, seem not to have enclosed some suburban areas that developed

during early Imperial times.[11] Inside one of these areas, nevertheless, was the Augustan theatre, which was soon dismantled and reused for the new defensive fortifications (as similarly happened at *Verona*, in the time of *Gallienus*).[12]

The city walls of Milan, capital of the Empire throughout the 4th century, were rebuilt at the time of *Maximian* and extended eastwards (fig.8), while at *Verona* they were reinforced with spur-shaped towers, possibly during the 5th century (fig.9a, b).[13]

Not every town, however, including the most important ones, was systematically characterised by such undertakings, as demonstrated, for example, by the southern enlargement towards the River *Ticino* of *Pavia*'s boundary walls, which seem to refer to the time of the Roman foundation rather than to Late Antiquity or the Gothic Age, as sometimes presumed.[14]

Furthermore, it must be remembered that a new system was developing at the time to defend the territory, specifically with the aforesaid *castra* (watching over the main cities, Milan, *Verona*),[15] and even exploiting other sites, such as *Lomello* (a rural village provided with imposing structures in the 5th century), that lay at strategic sites to control communications, and which therefore did at times have an 'urban-like' administrative role (*i.e. Castelseprio*).[16]

---

[8] As Brogiolo has observed (*Introduzione*, in Brogiolo 1999, p.12), it is uncertain whether every Pre-Alpine castle maintained its military role throughout the entire Longobard period, nevertheless a general abandonment of them is unlikely. A more peaceful period may have followed, especially in certain areas, considering that Paul the Deacon himself expressly mentions the strategic importance of most of those *castra* only for the span of years between 574-90, while, on the other hand, archaeology has not revealed new foundations (or rebuilding) in the Alpine and Pre-Alpine regions. The battlefield eventually shifted towards different geographical areas, such as *Friuli*, the northern *Adriatic* districts and along the main rivers of the *Po* Valley. Some indications in this sense would come from *Oderzo* and *Altino*, as well as from *Castrum Imolae*, the defensive structures of which seem to have been strengthened during the first period of the Longobard invasion.

[9] A clear example comes from *Rimini*, where archaeology has exposed some buildings placed as early as the 1st century AD against the city walls of Republican date (restored at the time of *Silla*), which had been largely demolished as a result of an evident loss of function; Ortalli, in Calbi – Susini 1995, p.516.

[10] Barnish, quoted by Brogiolo (*Conclusioni*, in Brogiolo 1995, p.239), rightly remarks that although the idea of an absolutely militarised society (as put forward for the Longobard period especially by the post-war historiography; see Chapter 1, note 12) should be played down, scholars should not underrate the warring element as a direct and essential cause of the organizational and political solutions of Late Antiquity as well the Early Middle Ages.

[11] Catarsi Dall'Aglio 1992, p.1. As often confirmed, the extension of the early-Imperial urban centres was usually too large, even when compared to the planning of the Tetrarchic-period towns which recovered after the crisis brought about by the century of military anarchy. The case of *Parma*, however, raises a difficulty as to interpretation, since no remains have been found relating to the supposed Augustan walls (Brogiolo – Gelichi 1998, p.57, who quote Dall'Aglio).

[12] Several examples attest to the use of imposing buildings, such as theatres or amphitheatres for different purposes, in particular relating to defensive structures (though sometimes the original role was not immediately lost, as was the case of *Volterra* or *Verona* itself). In the latter town, the amphitheatre was just 265 feet (80 m.) distant from the town circuit and 75 feet (23 m.) higher. This resulted in large-scale works to join the *circus* to the walls (at the time of *Gallienus*, as suggested by the archaeological data); Cavalieri Manasse – Hudson, in Brogiolo 1999, pp.71-72.

[13] The 'spur-shaped' towers, theorised by the Hellenistic *Poliorcetica* (art of siege warfare), were introduced to Italy by the Byzantines not earlier than the 5th century. According to this, scholars have put back into perspective the chronology of the city-walls of *Verona*, so that the second circle may probably date from the time of *Theodoric* rather than *Gallienus* (Cavalieri Manasse – Hudson, in Brogiolo 1999, p.71). Towers, built also with Roman stone, reinforced in the same way the enclosure walls at *Como*, even if the attribution to the 5th century or to the Byzantine period is not conclusive, have inclined to ascribe at least one of them to the 8th-9th century [after the studies carried out by Lusuardi Siena; in Brogiolo 1984, p.72]. Nonetheless, works of this kind would indicate a certain attention to wall maintenance and restoration, even during the very early Middle Ages (real constructions *ex novo* of the time have never been found by research).

[14] Peter Hudson has convincingly suggested that all the known features of the walls could be ascribed to the same building phase, possibly dating back to the time of the Roman colonization (1993, pp.108-09).

[15] Brogiolo, in Brogiolo 1999, p.13.

[16] *Ib.*, p.13. Archaeological investigations have proved that *Monte Barro* was operating from the years 320-420 (in the light of *sigillata* records), even if the high-density phases must have been at the time of the Greek-

Moreover, tasks of a political and control nature (in particular relevant to maritime connections) were also performed by those Byzantine *castra* that developed along the northern *Tyrrhenian* coasts (especially the *Maritima Italorum*). This could then provide a form of support for the towns as well as an organizational pattern for them.

An early example of meeting theses new military requirements is shown at *Susa*, where a small fortified site was adapted, with one end of the boundary walls incorporating two sides of the extant Roman enclosure. The work is dated to the time of the war between Constantine and *Maxentius*[17] and demonstrates the necessity to confine institutional buildings to more limited zones that were easier to administrate, and also the decline in urban standards of the early Roman Empire: several inhabited areas, which often developed on the outskirts and within town suburbs during the 1st and 2nd centuries, were usually excluded.[18]

An organizational system of this type develop at the time of the Greek-Gothic War and achieved its optimum efficiency during the struggles between Byzantines and Longobards. A clear example is at *Altino*, where ruins of walls found in the 1930s, probably related to a fortress dating to the years of the Germanic pressure upon the frontier near the River *Sele*.[19] Within the same geographical and chronological range the site of *Oderzo* can also be mentioned. Here the archaeology has brought to light remains of a fortification, a double-walled structure built with *opus-cementicium* technique in the inner side and reused stone materials in the foundation, which, according to the excavators, seem to have enclosed only a part of that town (this is supported, in particular, by the small width of the walls).[20]

In the *Abruzzi* region, in Byzantine contexts, imposing remains have also been discovered. These date to the 6th and early 7th centuries and are certainly related to defence purposes. At *Lanciano*, some structures were erected to protect certain areas of the ancient *municipium*, while at *Teramo*, a real *castrum* (called *Aprutiense*) was built to enclose part of the Roman centre (although using materials taken from the *Forum*).[21]

Such 'castles' were also built near urban sites (such as *Castrum ad Mare* close to *Pescara* and *St. Flaviani* near *Castrum Novum*),[22] a planning which appears to have similarly developed in Tuscany, where literary sources attest to a fortified location known as in *Prato Marzio*,[23] in a suburb of *Volterra*. In that region, moreover, the preservation of the original boundary walls, as well as the possibility of turning the ancient *acropolis* into a *castellum*, enabled towns like *Arezzo* (fig.10), *Chiusi* and *Fiesole* to have an important defensive role and take control of the main roads (especially those connecting Rome to *Ravenna*), and, what is more, to become fundamentally strong positions, in the 6th and 7th centuries, of either the strategic systems of the Byzantines or Longobards.[24]

Ciampoltrini has asserted that city walls represented a more significant element for town planning and life in the early Middle Ages (particularly the 6th-7th centuries)[25] than in Late Antiquity. Actually, the settlement patterns of the Longobards themselves, always trying to occupy the most important positions within the urban sites, especially during the first phase of the conquest, show a certain care for those areas close to defensive structures.

Scholars, however, mostly agree that the newcomers did upset the social order, but not really the planning. In fact, the context they found had ensued after a slow and differentiated process, started before, which had already broken up the classical city both in a material and ideal respect.

Such a transformation is marked, for instance, by the shift of political *foci*,[26] in particular the *forum*, which

---

Gothic War. Regarding other *castella* (particularly strategic sites such as *Belmonte* or *St. Giulio d'Orta*, besides the fortress of *Castelseprio*) the foundation date is commonly thought to have been around the middle of the 5th century. In conclusion, it can be noted that, after the 'hasty' arrangements of the early period, a well-planned system originated, 'tested' then since the years 450-90 (n.b. the final battle between *Odoacer* and *Theodoric* was fought at the very foot of *Monte Barro*).

[17] Archaeology supplies an *ante quem* date. The building, in fact, appears to have been constructed earlier than an arch of the baths ascribed to the time of *Gratianus* (AD 375-83); Brogiolo – Gelichi 1998, p.58 (also for a bibliographical reference to *Susa* and to its specific triangular plan which properly lent itself to the erection of a smaller and more protected area).

[18] Radical changes can also be observed in the main cities. In Milan the eastern extension of the *Maximian* walls must have plausibly been planned to enclose several built-up areas that developed outside the Late Republican period boundary; nevertheless some edifices placed in that district were demolished to make room for the urban baths (Caporusso 1991, p.356 and Brogiolo – Gelichi 1998, p.62). The city walls of *Ravenna*, probably erected at the same time (Christie, quoted by Brogiolo – Gelichi 1998, pp.62-64), around the very early 5th century, were considerably higher than the older defensive circuit. However they seem to have enclosed a rather limited political zone (for delegations *etc.*), in terms of the role of the new capital (most of the *domus* placed there was pulled down).

[19] Tirelli in Brogiolo 1995, pp.115-18.

[20] Castagna – Tirelli, in Brogiolo 1995, p.128.

[21] Real *castra* (inside the town) were also built at *Castrum Truentinum* (*Kastron Terentinon*), *Histonium* (*Kastron Reunia*) and *Castrum Novum* (*Kastron Nobo*). These constructions undoubtedly altered the ancient urban planning systems, even though they became a widespread feature, during the times of the Greek-Gothic war, as well as during the period when the Byzantines tried to hold the *Adriatic* coastal areas against the advance of the Longobards (Staffa, in Gelichi (ed.) 1997, p.71).

[22] *Conclusioni*, in Brogiolo 1995, p.241.

[23] In the absence of any archaeological evidence, scholars are uncertain whether it may be referred to as a Longobard centre: it was probably owned by the Treasury (and perhaps seat of *gastaldus*), since, after the fall of the Kingdom, the bishop was granted it (or came anyhow into its possession); Gelichi 1999, pp.80-81.

[24] Ciampoltrini, in Francovich – Noyè 1994, p.629 and 631.

[25] *Ib.*, pp.630-31.

[26] At *Brescia*, in the western quarter of the town (near the *Garza* rivulet), an example might be the so-called 'Winged Hall' (possibly a political seat during the Gothic period and *curia ducis* during the time of the Longobards). Judging from the materials and techniques, its

progressively lost its original function, as well as by the positioning of them in 'suburban' areas, especially near to the boundary walls, where also ecclesiastical buildings and production activities often settled.

Undoubtedly, strict control on these *foci* eventually represented for the invaders a top priority as much as the necessity to organize within limited and easy-to-defend fortified sites, an intent that can be clearly seen at *Lucca*, for example, which had redeveloped in the 4th century because of the presence of a state factory making weapons and as a result of imposing defensive structures.[27]

The first Germanic installation, in fact, according to some written sources, seems to have been arranged in the amphitheatre (as elsewhere), situated beyond the enclosure walls.[28] Although field-survey has only found curtain walls at the arcades, for defence requirements and dated to the time between the siege of *Narses* in 552 and the last decades of the 6th century, such evidence is remarkable, as the occupation of a strategic building for military reasons would also have given the possibility there of controlling the area of nearby *St. Frediano*, which had developed, after the recovery, with an important religious and economical role (fig.11a, b).

Excavation data from that zone have pointed out a certain initiative as is shown particularly by the Church of *St. Vincenzo* (following the typical model of the 5th-century *Po* Valley region) and by the restoration of the northern gate, where a building, interpreted either as 'service' or reinforcement work and dated to the 4th-5th century (on the basis of the pottery), was still built respecting the Roman planimetry.[29]

Gates had thus the primary function of linking town spaces to those that were *extra moenia* and, generally, to the region, which seems to have developed a diverse and stricter relationship with the different centres as early as the later Empire.[30] In fact, before the ecclesiastical

foundations, certain cities had 'encroached' upon some areas near their boundaries (and also beyond them), with several buildings, typically urban (such as *thermae*). This can be seen at *Volterra*, where the baths of *St. Felice* were arranged in the southern suburb, and at *Roselle*, where ruins of baths are close to the eastern gate and even further from its limits, in the plain towards *Grosseto* (at *Bagno di Roselle*; fig.12).[31]

An important element clearly relevant to the new situation that was taking place in town and rural contexts was the road network. This was still operating, usually maintained, and eventually protected from the sudden changes that resulted from topographical planning.[32]

Archaeology attests to a form of preservation and use of some roads, which (from a gate) went forward across the country. Examples, in particular, are towns such as *Lucca*, but also *Concordia*, where, similarly, the strategic role and presence of a state factory entailed the maintenance of at least the main communications. At *Concordia* the extension of the *decumanus maximus* was connected with the *Via Annia*, and therefore with the *metropolis* of *Aquileia*. Therefore its existence and use, proved for the 4th-5th centuries by the disposition of some *necropolises*, possibly lasted up to the 6th century, when the well-known floods, and other events, brought about also the abandonment of that town itself (fig.13).[33]
As for the urban streets, a certain continuity can be seen. This reflects a rare element of stability within the framework of several changes, especially from Tuscany, until the middle centuries of early Middle Ages (Gelichi)[34] (fig.14).

---

restoration (specifically the *portico* and colonnade) may have eventually occurred at the same time as the reconstruction of the city walls (which encompass it exactly). Both works may be plausibly ascribed (following the literary sources also) to the Gothic Age. Alternatively, if the palace were older, it would be noteworthy that its importance compelled (in order to enclose and so defend it) the extension of the circuit and a huge embankment of the *Garza*. Brogiolo 1993, pp.58-65.

[27] The restoration of the Republican era *opus-quadratum* wall circuit was fundamental for the military role of the fortress-town of *Lucca*, held by the time of *Probus*. This work, still described as impenetrable in the late 6th century (*Agazia*), must have survived throughout the Longobard period; indeed, some parts of it survived until the 13th century; (Ciampoltrini, in Francovich – Noyé 1994, p.616 and Ciampoltrini – Notini 1990, pp.561-64).

[28] Gelichi 1999, p.34.

[29] *Ib.*, pp.27-29; see also *infra* note 35 for the production works arranged on Imperial structures.

[30] The constant demand for timber by the *fabrica* of *Lucca* was likely to have been the main reason for the recovery of the surrounding territory, as shown by the large rise in the number of settlements over the low

valley of the River *Serchio* in the 4th and 5th centuries (Ciampoltrini – Notini 1990, p.590).

[31] Among others, a reference for *Volterra* is to be found in Ricci, *Volterra tra Tardoantico e Alto medioevo*, 'Archeologia Medievale' XXI, 1994, p.639 and 640 (fig.1); about *Roselle*, Gelichi 1999, p.109 and pl. IV.

[32] Some ancient streets fell into neglect, as can be noted, for instance, at *Luni* or *Cosa*, between Late Antiquity and the early centuries of the Middle Ages. Concerning this, geomorphologic changes did contribute to the disuse of whole route systems, but the political and economic weakness of such centres should also be considered, once they had become peripheral (not linked to the new main routes) and unable to keep the efficiency of their infrastructures; Gelichi 1999, p.138. On the contrary, quite a different situation existed in more thriving cities, where a less decline in road-maintenance seems to have occurred. Although, for economic reasons, also in early Imperial times, there was a large difference between major and secondary roads in terms of building and upkeep. In *Bologna*, for example, the importance of certain streets is attested by several restoration works dating from Late Antiquity to the Early Medieval period. Nonetheless, 'makeshift' solutions (small repairs, ballast of *cocciopesto*, crushed shards) show a sharp fall in technique, as is also witnessed at *Classe*, at least until the end of the 7th or beginning of the 8th century. Ortalli 1984, specifically pp.391-92.

[33] About *Lucca*, Gelichi 1999, pl. III (p.29) and pl. IV (p.33); for *Concordia*, Croce Da Villa 1987, p.86.

[34] *Considerazioni conclusive*, in Gelichi 1999, p.136. At *Pistoia*, in the area near the Bishop's Palace, the major road of Late Antique planning survived (although rather dilapidated) until the advanced early Middle Ages (phases VIII-IX). In addition, its layout was still taken into account by the works carried out from the 9th to 11th centuries, specifically the erection of a tower and afterwards the bishop's residence (the latter, however, seems to have caused that to be

The *cardus* and *decumanus* on the one hand, and the main country-roads on the other, naturally met each other at the town gates, which were becoming, as mentioned above, important places of cohesion, considering that cult and production centres had developed nearby.

Such a consequence also seems to have characterised those structures (and the areas close to them) throughout the early Middle Ages, and not only in Late Antiquity, when the development of buildings (especially religious ones) on the fringe of cities could have eventually marked an 'improvised or temporary' status, before the possibility of occupying more central and active zones. At *Lucca*, for example, near to the northern access, manufacturing probably continued into the 7th-8th centuries, as the four gates, on the basis of 8th- and 9th-century literary sources, appeared to have been named after the respective suburban churches and situated in bustling quarters that had a certain social importance.[35] On the other hand, the loss of functionality that occurred at times to the boundary walls in very Early Medieval times (*i.e.*, in Milan)[36] must not always have meant the decay of the whole structure concerned, nor the marginalization of the areas close by. At *Trent*, for example, near to the *Porta Veronensis*, some of the chief public buildings would have been erected in the late Middle Ages (Municipal Tower and Magistrate's Palace).[37]

During Late Antiquity (and the centuries of transition) there was a tendency, within the urban limits, towards the development of smaller complexes, marked by either economic, political or cult/religious features, which brought about the 'patchwork' planning, often pointed out by scholars as typical of Early Medieval towns.[38]
In the light of this, it would be not suitable to consider enclosure walls as inseparable structures interacting in the same way with all the districts. The practice of settling smaller sites, in fact, might have possibly implied only the use and restoration of specific parts of them, whilst others would have even resulted as quite marginal events.

Moreover, works such as repairs or additions, eventually intended to create or enclose new areas,[39] should be seen as remarkable changes of the relationship between the ancient spaces themselves – rather than as an unquestionable contraction of cities (also considering the increasing importance of some suburban areas).[40]

The well-known *topos* of contraction is not likely, therefore, to fully describe the Early Medieval town, firstly because it would mean starting from standards peculiar to the Republican era, lost for centuries, as well as the idea itself of Roman planning.[41] What is more, because most of the works in question eventually seem seldom, if ever, to be more recent than the Gothic period.[42]

Ward Perkins has observed that the building of city walls was probably not widespread throughout the Early Middle Ages,[43] as both the Longobards and Carolingians apparently did not spend large sums on such undertakings. The structures inherited from the Roman and Late Antique past were evidently enough to provide an adequate defensive system, which, on the basis of the available archaeological data, never entailed construction *ex novo*. Apart from maintenance, limited works, at most, have been found – either to enclose newly developed areas of some political importance, or to undertake works on imposing ancient monuments (baths, theatres, amphitheatres), which could have been easily used during any siege (as was the case at *Benevento*).[44]

progressively blocked and totally removed); Vannini 1985, pp.59 and 64. In conclusion, another example would be in Rome, where not only the ancient road network, but even the old material structures themselves often survived (Brogiolo – Gelichi 1998, p.165). The streets leading to the *Esquiline* were kept almost intact up until the 8th century (as is also attested to by the Anonymous of *Einsiedeln*); Bianchi, in Gelichi (ed.) 1997, p.89.

[35] Ciampoltrini – Notini 1990, pp.585 and 591; Gelichi 1999, p.33.

[36] In that city, the Monastery of *St. Maria di Aurona* was placed against the surrounding walls (8th-century), and a tower was even made over its use (Brogiolo – Gelichi 1998, pp.73-74, who also mention other references).

[37] In the 4th-5th centuries the gate structures were used as occasional shelter and the poor materials found there mirror well the general crisis of that town. Nevertheless, the later building of an imposing wall on the outer side would seem to indicate continuous (defensive?) function, while the arrangement of the area as a cemetery (not dated exactly, but to be referred to the second half of the first millennium AD) may be more connected with the important religious complex erected nearby, where the present cathedral was also eventually built; Baggio Bernardoni 1997, pp.239-40.

[38] See, for example, Brogiolo 1987, in particular pp.38-41.

[39] *I.e.*, *Brescia*, where the construction of a wall (roughly dating to Late Antiquity) was possibly intended to enclose the southernmost limit of the area, which has been assumed as a demesne in Longobard times; Brogiolo 1993, pp.52-55.

[40] An example is the known complex of *St. Vincenzo* at *Lucca* as well as, at *Bologna*, the *extra urbem* district where the Monastery of *St. Stefano* will then have been erected (Brogiolo – Gelichi 1998, p.56). At *Benevento*, the circle of walls, probably rebuilt by *Arechi II*, certainly left out southern and western quarters of the Roman town (Rotili 1986, p.87), but it was also extended, enclosing the area called '*Civitas Nova*' (Brogiolo – Gelichi 1998, p.68-72).

[41] The Longobards themselves, when necessary, usually took up a defensive position within tight and well-protected spaces, showing indifference towards the locals and the surrounding built-up areas (typical of invaders, especially during the early stages of a conquest; Gasparri, in Brogiolo 1995, p.10). On the other hand this reflected a diverse and partial approach to urban space, mostly intended as an agglomeration of strategic places to be controlled. This is perhaps the reason they chose to settle in *Fiesole* instead of Florence, which, although equally important in a military sense, should have been more difficult to manage (as regards defence) because of the existence of the entire Republican era circuit. Ultimately it must be remembered that even the Byzantines contributed to the disruption of the ancient planning by means of *castra* built inside several centres (Staffa, in Gelichi [ed.] 1997, p.72).

[42] The selenite walls of *Bologna* have for a long time been a *vexata quaestio*, in particular concerning the supposed contraction of that town. However, they seem more convincingly to date back to the second half of the 5th century, following an earlier suggestion of Fasoli, rather than to an earlier time (3rd/4th century, as in Brogiolo – Gelichi 1998, pp.55-56); Gelichi 1998, p.84 (note 25, where previous assertions are revisited).

[43] 1984, p.198.

[44] These *additamenta* (*opus incertum* constructions, reinforced with large stones, especially at the bottom of the structure) were ordered,

Scholars are usually wary of ascribing huge works to the first centuries of the Early Middle Ages, because of the scant interest sometimes given to such structures throughout the period concerned[45] and, not considering ecclesiastical foundations, because only in the true Carolingian period was a good level generally achieved in architectural planning and technique (however it was city-state policy that dictated and redrew boundaries and town-planning).

Furthermore, in some cases, as a result of new careful surveying, some hypotheses regarding presumed *additamenta* have been put back into perspective (as at *Lucca*, where the supposed 7th-century north-western enlargement appears to belong to the original enclosure instead; fig.11a, b);[46] Some caution seems therefore to be required, even confirmation amongst written sources seems to exist. In fact, although 10th-century literary evidence, asserting the construction of the city walls of *Salerno* by *Arechis II* is considered reliable (although there is a lack of clear material proof),[47] a review of some documents from *Pisa*, for example, has suggested new considerations about the defensive structures of that Tuscan town.

Old hypotheses proposed that certain boundaries mentioned in a charter of Conrad the Second (1027) would have been part of an Early Medieval construction, which should have marked a sure reduction of the late Roman limits, in particular, in the eastern zone, where the toponym *Civitas vetera* should refer to the area left out (fig.15). On the contrary, recent studies suggest not only that this district might have been extra-urban as early as Roman times, but that the date of the fortified structure is 5th-century (especially in the light of its relationship with the bishop's residence on the north-western side. Apart from the clear archaeological evidence, its priority appears reasonable, since, as shown also from other contexts, the bishop would have hardly left his building out of the enclosure if it had been erected after).[48]

At *Reggio Emilia*, during an excavation carried out in 1980-81, a section of wall was discovered (rubble work, filled with river pebbles fixed with poor mortar, preserved only in the foundation), the construction of which seems, however, to date probably back to Late Antiquity. A similar find was also unearthed in 1997 in the same town, very close to the Monastery of *St. Tommaso*. The latter is taken as being part of the boundary walls mentioned in Early Medieval written accounts, whereas this is not supported in the former discovery.[49]

Finally, and not related to the defensive enclosure in question, there is the example of the structure excavated during a survey led by Siliprandi in 1935. This work is referred to the fortification proposed by Bishop Peter (about 900), for the protection of the area around his residence. This construction is also attested by written sources, as, for example, a charter issued by the Emperor, who granted the aforesaid prelate to enclose '*dictam ecclesiam suam per girum suae potestatis*'. Furthermore, a similar undertaking has a documented comparison at *Modena*, where *Leodoinus* was allowed in 891 to build a boundary structure not longer than a mile.[50] Archaeological evidence from the not much later *Castrum* of *St. Cassiani* (a see of *Imola*'s diocese; suburban from the 9th-10th century), which, nevertheless, seems to just have been protected by a roughly 20 ft. (6 m.) wide, 7 ft. (about 2 m.) deep moat, at least in the first phase (according to a pattern typical of several plain sites of the time).[51]

These examples possibly represent clear matches of the general development of fortifications around episcopal buildings, the most striking of which must surely be the walls of the Vatican.

That work, demonstrating advanced techniques, was ordered by Pope *Leo IV*. These walls are not just to be interpreted as a defensive construction (brought about by sudden dangers, such as '*mali cristiani*'[52] or Saracens – who plundered St. Peter's in 846, under his predecessor *Sergius II*), but also as part of an improving activity fostered by the Papacy, particularly throughout the 9th century, intended to reorganize the country planning of the Region *Latium* itself (*i.e.*, by means of urban

---

according to tradition, by *Arechi II* (758-87); Rotili 1986, pp.145, 149, followed by Brogiolo – Gelichi 1998, p.72. An interesting parallel may be drawn with works to some great Roman monuments beginning from the second half of the 3rd century (a clear example from *Verona*, since the time of *Probus*, see *infra* note 12).

[45] *Ib.*, p.73.

[46] Gelichi 1999, pp.27-28.

[47] Delogu 1977, p.16 (quoted by Brogiolo – Gelichi 1998, p.72).

[48] This is the convincing thesis advanced by Gelichi (*Le mura inesistenti e la città dimezzata...*, 1998, pp.75-88). According to the previous idea of Violante, the Late Roman boundary of that town (before contraction) would have been indicated by the '*murum veterem*' mentioned in the document above-cited. It also appears in two other charters but, significantly, never connected with the circuit. If those attested to by the toponym '*Supracastello*' were accepted as parts of the wall in question (as suggested by Garzella 1990, pp.9-10), one could imagine a long building (uncertainly interpreted) crossing the eastern suburban area (Roman aqueduct?). Alternatively, Redi explains the term '*castellum*' as an ancient edifice redesigned for defensive purposes during the Early Middle Ages – eventually the Longobard period (Roman *circus*?, since some remains have curvilinear shapes); Redi 1991, p.82.

[49] Gelichi (ed.), *Archeologia medievale in Emilia occidentale. Ricerche e studi*, 1998, p.12. A paper of AD 835 locates the complex of *St. Tommaso* just outside the urban boundary (therefore quite nearby); a difficulty may be eventually raised whether the aforesaid remains had belonged to the city walls, considering their width of 5 ft. (1.5 m.), if it is the complete measure). At *Oderzo*, in fact, a structure of the same size has been ascribed by excavators to a *castrum* built inside the town, since supposed too small for the main circuit. These two contexts should have similar standards, as, to judge from 5th- and 6th-century pottery finds, they must have been roughly contemporaneous: see *infra* text and note 20).

[50] *Ib.*, p.12 and Gelichi, in Francovich – Noyé 1994, pp.575-76.

[51] Brogiolo – Gelichi 1998, p.73.

[52] Gelichi (ed.), *Archeologia medievale in Emilia...*, 1998, p.12 (quoting from Settia).

foundations). Moreover, such an undertaking definitely recalls important state prerogatives, and thus it could well represent a clear sign of the transfer of the Roman duchy from Byzantine authority to the rising papal rule.[53]

In conclusion, on the one hand, the possession of the *munus fortificandi* elevated the bishop of Rome among the highest of the public hierarchs (such as the *princeps Romanorum* or the Emperor), whereas, on the other, the impression of strict control over that right by the ecclesiastical institution illustrates fight for power between the Pope and the aristocracy of the time. Considering the unrest and riotous nobles of 8th- and 9th-century Rome,[54] a 'militarised' context should be expected, but the sole defensive structures of *Castrum Aurum* cannot really support any interpretation in this sense; this is also indicated by the archaeological survey of the mid- to late-Carolingian high-status houses at the *Nerva Forum*.[55] Current research still lacks the essential data to help understand the reasons why the elite did not build private castles. Nevertheless, the different junctures of the further developments (changes in the balance of power, liberty of the aristocracy?), when the erection of towers also marked the social rise of families, such as the *Stefaneschi-Ildebrandi*, the *de Papa*, and the *Frangipane*. 11th-century archaeological evidence has revealed the significant residence of the latter on the *Palatine*, even though it occupies the most peripheral areas of the Hill, far from the ancient political buildings and watching over the main roads.[56]

## 2.3. Urban planning and building.

In Late Antiquity city walls particularly drew the public attention of the authorities, especially because of the more urgent defence requirements and the ensuing military institutions that increasingly featured town and country planning. *Ravenna*'s fortifications, for example, dating back to the early 5th century, were undoubtedly one of the greatest building projects of the time, both in

terms of their scale and expense.[57] However the differences in the use of materials and construction, compared to the more 'classical' methods, illustrate the changes over the centuries – not least in terms of the decline in technical know-how, as sometimes emerges with rushed work, possibly consequent on sudden events or emergencies. (Noteworthy, in this sense, is the stratigraphical sequence of the enclosure walls found at *Urbino*. After the accurate Republican period *opus quadratum*, and the third-century brickwork, a sixth-century 'chaotic' phase can be distinguished by the reuse of material, poorly fixed and plastered. This well reflects what *Procopius* wrote about *Belisarius*, who was in a hurry to restore the defensive structures of that town in 545).[58]

Written sources often stress on dramatic situations, in particular during the Greek-Gothic War, when the necessity to shelter rural populations or to quarter troops called for measures that would have greatly affected urban housing and planning, as, for example, with the occupation of public areas or the partition of several *domus*, because of lack of space.[59]

The consequences of such military events, although definitely burdensome, must however be viewed in the light of wider changes that began to develop as early as the Tetrarchic era (as already seen before in terms of trading and production[60]), when various strategic solutions had already implied a diverse kind of control over the territory to cope with a new political and geographical situation, which, moreover, had caused some regions, especially in the north of the peninsula, to become border zones once more.[61]

The different (probably reduced) resource allocation that followed brought about, and also interacted with, considerable social-economic changes which undoubtedly did not occur evenly and thus had not the same effect within each context,[62] although they do reflect some common traits, such as the decline in technical quality or general level of building investment.

The political and administrative course of Late Antiquity, mostly because of military requirements, 'selected' just a few of the secondary urban sites (as emerges from the decay or lack of management of their infrastructures), and certainly becoming a catalyst leading to crises within those towns that had already lost their original role years previously and had continued and/or slowed down their decline, at least until the mid-Empire era, only because of the well-organised and strongly centralised Roman

---

[53] The stages of the process, which will bring the Church fully to achieve temporal power, can also be revealed by the activities promoted by the Pope during the first half of the 8th century, when the severance of relations with the Eastern Roman Empire was about to be finalized. Restoration works at the *Aurelian* circuit, attributed to *Sisinnius* (708), and Gregory the Second (715) by the *Liber Pontificalis*, as well as the rebuilding of the enclosure walls at *Centumcellae*, ordered by Gregory the Third (731-41), might actually be interpreted in the light of a political claim as well (if we take into account that the boundary walls also had a symbolic meaning and lay strictly within the competence of the State; notwithstanding, even in the *Corpus Iuris*, the bishop, with three other *principales*, was already expected to supervise works of this kind); Marazzi, in Francovich – Noyé 1994, in particular p.255 and foll. (and note 17). The fortifications promoted by *Arechi II* (*infra*, text and notes 44, 47) may also be considered in this sense – a show of authority indeed, while the Longobards in the north were about to be finally defeated by the Carolingians (*ib.*, pp.272-73).

[54] Manacorda – Marazzi – Zanini, in Francovich – Noyé 1994, p.652.

[55] Meneghini – Santangeli Valenzani 1996, pp.83-84.

[56] Augenti, in Francovich – Noyé 1994, pp.686-87.

[57] Parenti, in Brogiolo 1994, p.30.

[58] Luni – Ermeti, in Gelichi (ed.) 1997, pp.41-42.

[59] At *Pavia* they were turned into *angustissimi tuguri* (real holes) at the time of the war between *Theodoric* and *Odoacer*, as reported by *Ennodius* (*Vita Epiphani*, p.98,15, quoted by Brogiolo 1993, p.73).

[60] See Chapter 1, final remarks.

[61] Brogiolo – Gelichi 1998, p.59.

[62] Parenti, in Brogiolo 1994, p.25.

system. The early decline of the cities in southern *Piedmont* has comparisons with the 2nd-3rd century cyclic recession that took place over most of central and northern Italy (*i.e.*, in Tuscany). However the non-resettlement and non-recovery of the abandoned sites should rather indicate a real failure, notwithstanding an attempt to balance out the demographic element and the number of towns (after the over-urbanization of that region during the Roman colonization),[63] yet at the time of the Roman advance, the southern *Etrurian* cities were strongholds set against the Etruscan sites of the north. Nevertheless, once the conquest was accomplished, several difficulties were apparent from as far back as Augustan times, and most had collapsed since the 5th century (even though some would have played an important role for *Byzantium* within the connections between *Latium* and *Maritima Italorum*).[64]

Finally, the *Abruzzi* region represents a clear example of such development, as shown, in particular, by the sharp difference between inland- and coast sites, the latter being the only ones to hold their position within a trading network that tended to distribute merchandise through markets usually managed by the largest landowners.[65] Not only poorer materials, such as earth/clay, and building techniques such as dry-walling (instead of mortar) were used again in many hinterland towns (more typical of the prehistoric culture or, in any case, more associated with rural building at least until mid-Empire times). However most of these towns also lost quite early their urban features, and became to resemble villages within the limits of the ancient cities.[66]

Consequently, four *municipia*, situated in the hinterland (*Amiternum, Reate, Interamnia, Aveia*; fig.16) were as

early as AD 325 under the care of *C. Sallius Sofronius Pompeianus*, a fact that throws some light on the eventual possibilities of restoration or preservation of a certain *decorum* offered by landowners' patronage (belonging to the senatorial class)[67] and that also has comparisons elsewhere, and among contemporaneous contexts. At *Volterra*, the construction of *Vallebuona*'s baths was ordered by the *Petronii Volusiani*, nevertheless, instead of being part of a form of planning project aimed at recovering that town, it could be seen rather as a work to celebrate the aforementioned family's entrance into the Senate (at the time of *Probus*). In the same way, at *Roselle*, the *Bassii Basilica* was originally a public building but, after it had been restored by that family in the 2nd/3rd century, it became a monument to the glory of that *gens*.

At this point, it is worth remembering the development of privatization (Citter) fostered by the authorities, by means of granting private citizens state areas and thereby intending to preserve some from decay (despite their earlier institutional/political importance).[68] The loss of functionality that occurred to the ancient administrative buildings seems much more marked during the transition centuries and their marginalization (or transformation)[69] is the most striking evidence of either the alteration or fall of the classic city model (as is also evident from archaeological surveys about housing).

From a few well-studied examples in Lombardy and *Emilia Romagna* come certain data that can be reasonably extended to other areas of the peninsula (especially central and northern). However, as already said, these should be dealt with cautiously, particularly with regard to the chronological sequence, which, over different periods (but generally between the 4th and 5th/6th centuries), brought to an end the large single family *domus* system, when new production and settlement patterns appear to have already taken place.[70] What is particularly striking is the diverse use of these buildings

---

[63] La Rocca, in Francovich – Noyé 1994, p.550.

[64] Despite several efforts of *curatores* (at *Saturnia* urban landowners) during the 3rd and 4th centuries to recover from disruptions, centres such as *Cosa, Saturnia* and *Heba* progressively lost their main urban characteristics (in the case of *Cosa*, even after it had been unsuccessfully refounded and renamed *Ansedonia* by the Byzantines); on the other hand, some continuation in this sense can be noted at *Roselle, Populonia* and *Sovana* (although affected by change and deterioration), where, between the 5th and 7th centuries, even bishop's sees were established; Gelichi 1999, pp.133-34.

[65] Staffa rightly calls the Late Antiquity of *Abruzzi* the era of large landed estates (as shown by the great variety and high quality of pottery coming from the excavations of many rural *villae*, compared with the very poor finds from certain towns, especially in inland areas); Staffa, in Gelichi (ed.) 1997, p.71.

[66] *Ib.*, pp.73-74. Poor rustic building techniques emerge also from the most thriving towns on the coast, whose planning often reflected the dramatic events of the period (at *Castrum Truentinum*, for example, some storehouses placed in the ex-commercial quarter were partitioned and rearranged as compact accommodation in the second half of the 4th century). Nevertheless, because of their strategic-economic role, centres such as *Pescara* maintained a certain urban status throughout the Byzantine period and seem to have been on the rise since the 9th century (from that time date considerable rebuilding works at the dockyard). On the other hand, the inland regions appear to have based their economy on rural activities typical of Prehistoric contexts, such as, transhumance. There are interesting parallels with Braudel's long-lasting courses (that can generally be observed when social and economic factors are weaker); Braudel 1982, vol. I, p.74 and foll.

[67] Staffa (see note 65 for the reference concerned), p.71.

[68] Citter, in Gelichi (ed.) 1997, pp.27-28 (also for *Volterra* and *Roselle*). Private building too was also affected at the same time by deterioration (as attested to by the Justinian code as well as by the *Diocletian* and *Maximian* laws). The state might well have restored a *domus* if abandoned or in ruins and taken possession of it if the lawful owner had not refunded the expenses within the prescribed term. According to a law promulgated by *Alexander Severus* in AD 224 the lots concerned could even have been transformed into gardens with the neighbours' consent (the early date is interesting); Meneghini – Santangeli Valenzani 1996, p.68.

[69] Among several examples, there is the forum at *Luni*, by then in a state of decay and which was settled by wooden huts in the 6th century; at Florence the forum became a market square (until the 10th century), while at *Lucca* and *Volterra* two churches dedicated to *St. Michele* (called indeed *in foro*) were built on it; Gelichi 1999, p.135.

[70] While in *Emilia-Romagna* the *domus* system seems to have come to an end in the 3rd and 4th century as a result of the first barbarian raids (Catarsi Dall'Aglio, p.149 and Gelichi, p.158, both in Brogiolo 1994), in Rome the so-called 'small *Domus*' of *Piazza dei Cinquecento* shows the earliest signs of decay only in layers of the second half of the 5th and the beginning of the 6th century (Meneghini – Santangeli Valenzani, pp.53 and foll., bibliographical reference at note 68).

(if not exploited as quarries), over which were often built workshops, churches, even baths (for example at *Ravenna*):[71] in any event, where the structures were rearranged as dwellings the differences between these latter and the previous forms are especially noticeable (above all from the widespread use of wood, or the technological background and knowledge of its use).

Whilst timber would have been the prevailing material (if not the only one) during the Longobard age (although not exclusively in the regions directly subjected to Germanic influence),[72] wood, used with stone, was also employed during Gothic times, and was largely used for many construction solutions – roofing, wall-coverings, floorings, partitions (creating open-plan halls generally with their own hearths placed directly on the ground). Further developments in building styles appeared gradually; often the orientation of previous residences was maintained, whereas the external walls were eventually reused as part of the standing framework, becoming, after a rise in floor level, the foundations, into which load-bearing wooden posts were driven directly.[73]

What emerges from the decline in construction standards and from the partitioning (sometimes into very narrow structures) is that the new residents had limited resources: they probably came from other social classes, considering their ways of settling and, above all, they had a different concept of space.[74] Amongst the examples of *via Alberto Mario* at *Brescia* (fig.17) and the houses in *via Dante* at *Verona*, alignments were generally kept (especially those close to the road), nevertheless, the exploitation of less rooms and the arrangement of *domus* halls like the *portico* or the peristyle as abode seriously mark a big change, within a development widely spread, although its causes and consequences are not completely clear.[75]

Some hypotheses have been put forward to explain it, as, for instance, parcelling-outs in result of inheritance dividing-up, urgent necessity to quarter troops and, last but not least, the coming of numbers of rural people to the town, ensued from a growing unstable and insecure situation, which must have actually been harmful to the agricultural production system (and so to the urban economy itself too):[76] this could well account for poorer habits and technical backgrounds, certainly belonging to prehistoric tradition, as long-outcast and typical of fringe-areas as getting on again during "weak" periods or junctures.

At the same time cultural reasons are also advanced, to be undoubtedly considered as regards those contexts where the presence of foreign people should have affected both building know-hows and settlement patterns;[77] despite this, social and economical causes seem however to have been more conclusive, as it would be attested too by the dramatic involution of urban infrastructures, which indicates short service provisions as well as a sharp worsening of city-management-machinery: by the third century, in fact, progressively although in different ways depending on districts, excavations regularly find partially uninhabited areas used as dumping ground, being this a clear sign that waste-collection and -disposal systems were hardly in working order (while sometimes a collapse of sewerage systems really did occur).[78] The same difficulties (or at least a break from the previous organization) appear also to have hit the water supply, since the few repairs and restorations of Roman aqueducts, usually due to exceptional circumstances, seem to have often been carried out after rather a long

---

[71] Gelichi, in Brogiolo 1994, p.158.

[72] In addition to the wooden structure, another pattern possibly recalling influence of regions beyond the Alps is represented by sunken huts. Such typological solutions may also be referred to prehistoric models, as it mostly appears as consequent on adaptation to humid climate (it is quite common, in fact, over several zones of Europe). This idea seems to be backed by the Byzantine *grubenhäuser* brought to light in *Apulia*; Arthur 1999, pp.171-78.

[73] Such solutions have been found during many excavations in *Piedmont*, even if (at *Vercelli*) the ancient walls had been maintained but, without any clear reason, not exploited; Wataghin, in Brogiolo 1994, pp.97-98. A gradual change can be observed in the *Abruzzi* region too (*Pescara*, *Truentum*), where, throughout the 5th and 6th century, wooden constructions took the place of often crumbling stone buildings; Staffa, in Brogiolo 1994, pp.70-71.

[74] Consequent on the different ways of settlement, compared to the Roman ones, the research has often big difficulties in locating and discovering Early Medieval structures: at *Vercelli*, for instance, during an excavation on a central quarter of the town, a lot of pottery shards had been firstly dug out, whilst only further surveying succeeded to realize the existence of the relating dwelling houses (Wataghin, in Brogiolo 1994, p.93, note 40).

[75] Another well-known example comes from the excavation of *Palazzo Tabarelli* at *Trento* (Brogiolo 1993, pp.74-82); it is interesting that (as checked in *via A. Mario*'s building) the floors seem to have been often maintained at the Roman-Age level for a long time, whilst they appear as considerably risen only in the early Longobard layers.

[76] A reference is Brogiolo – Gelichi 1998, p.157.

[77] The Region of Upper *Adige/Süd Tirol* is of interest (*i.e. Villandro*; however, not necessarily supporting the idea of new people); the wide use of ballast (after the last desertion occurred in the 6th century) seems to have characterised especially those sites which had been previously settled during the Roman Age (but not for others where they would have also been beneficial, given the same climatic [humid] conditions). This may also explain the obliteration of the ancient heathen culture, since the Roman structures could have been easily reused (still in a good state of repair and definitely superior to the following constructions); Dal Ri – Rizzi, in Brogiolo 1994, pp.137-39.

[78] Organic waste dumping and decomposition could have been among the causes of the so-called 'dark earth', although several difficulties generally come up when any specific phenomenon (or even more than one at the same time) is singled out (and scholars therefore are still debating the matter). At urban sites, evidence in this sense is usually recorded when dealing with the transitional layers between the Roman and Early Medieval phases and differently interpreted as decomposition of structures built with perishable materials (charcoal is often found), alluvial deposits, as well as the organic waste, easily explainable considering the dramatic deficiency of Early Medieval drainage systems. Nevertheless, the unexpected presence of dark earths in certain places prevents us from strictly ascribing them either to specific chronological contexts or to limited geographical areas, or, moreover, to particular climatic conditions, as is proposed by some French scholars (this phenomenon, in fact, seems to have affected cities that had not really 'deteriorated', i.e. Rome and Naples, while at *Lucca*, it even concerns mid-Imperial phases, as well as 11th-century layers, definitely indicated by a rising urban recovery). Brogiolo – Gelichi 1998, pp.90-95.

period of inactivity, whilst the utilization of them, not certain after the 7th century, probably refers to ecclesiastical sites, generally concerning clergy *balnea* or monastery baths.[79] Finally, in relation to road networks, among a good number of them there the continuity of the ancient system survived until the mid-Early Middle Ages (despite an inferior maintenance);[80] nevertheless, there are contrary examples too (*i.e.*, at *Roselle* the *cardo* was clogged in part as early as the end of the 4th century, and the *decumanus* was neglected by the 6th century). Moreover, as Citter remarks, the survival of a street could have been the result of a new road which kept the connexion between two existing gates, but not necessarily the previous Roman layout.[81]

Amongst some contexts a remarkable recovery developed, although chronologically and geographically limited, the result of particular conditions as, for example, the raising of Milan to the role of capital, which must have definitely had a positive influence on the planning of that city: in the area of the present *Piazza Duomo*, a two-hundred-year-old residence was then restored at the beginning of the 5th century by the construction of new halls set around a courtyard and provided with a heating system, whereas at the time of *Theodoric* some crushed pot-shard (*cocciopesto*) floors were rebuilt and a *portico* erected along the road, paved with recycled slabs (the presence of a well means that the aqueduct nearby did not work). However, decay must have been imminent by the mid-6th century (as the hypocaust fell into disuse and rubbish was dumped on the ground), being by then, almost crumbling, replaced by Longobard-Age wooden huts.[82]

Such a recovery should have eventually been consequent on Milan's political status, since a considerable urbanistic reorganization was carried out also in *Ravenna* throughout the 5th and 6th centuries, as it itself held the same role. The construction of residences with apsidal halls (probably also intended for civic functions) shows court-building models, which, as far as regards their cost and care, should be still ascribed to classical tradition, as emerges, at the same time, from the revived care of infrastructures, like the aqueduct, baths, roads and port (*Classe*).[83]

The good influence of the capital positively affected most of the *Romagna* Region, especially the eastern part

(largely checked by archaeological surveys),[84] even though the '*elan vital*' seems to have faded as early as Gothic times, and not to be interpreted, therefore, as a real and lasting reversal of the trend.[85] The famous *Papyrus Tjaeder* from *Ravenna* (describing a home sale through a banker, *Teodorus argentarius*) could well reflect a type of residence that was possibly being built by the beginning of the Early Middle Ages. It was a two-storeyed building, the *portico* made with bricks (the material used for the rest of the structures is not known). However the co-ownership and sharing of the well, and, above all, the fact that the deal concerned only a part of the estate appear in sharp contrast to the magnificence of the previous period.[86]

Furthermore, the house of the *Papyrus* finds matches both archaeological – for example the rearrangement for dwelling of the dock depots carried out at that time at *Classe* (fig.18) – and documented, as, among the written sources of a couple of centuries later, a similar pattern is largely attested as well as one completely undertaken in timber.[87]

This latter style was relatively widespread throughout central and northern Italy, so it could eventually mean that typological and technical differences were becoming fewer between the *Romania* and *Langobardia* Regions in the mid-Early Middle Ages (as is also reflected in pottery artefacts). The use of wood in place of stone had developed during the centuries of transition but, whilst the Germanic influence seems to have affected more conclusively districts such as Lombardy (as regards in particular minor buildings), the Byzantine areas were characterised by a slower progression, phases of which can possibly be pointed out in the presence of wooden huts close to more impressive stone/masonry constructions, such as cathedrals (at *Luni*; fig.19b) or boundary walls (around the *castrum* of *St. Antonino di Perti*; fig.19a).[88]

---

[79] *Ib.*, pp.76-77, 83.

[80] See *infra* note 32.

[81] Hard to establish without clear archaeological data (Citter, in Gelichi [ed.] 1997, p.28); for *Roselle*'s road-network also Gelichi 1999, p.136.

[82] Other noteworthy restoration examples come from *via Tommaso Grossi*, as well as from *Piazza Rosate* at *Bergamo*, eventually consequent on the positive influence of the capital; Brogiolo 1996, p.79 (about Milan, he follows Perring, in Caporusso 1991).

[83] The archaeological find of some lead *fistulae* (pipes) may support the restoration of town waterworks ordered by *Theodoric* in the years 502-03 (as attested by *Cassiodorus*); Brogiolo – Gelichi 1998, p.76.

[84] High-quality brick buildings (with mosaic [at times *sectile*] floors), placed around a large courtyard, have been exposed at *Faenza*, *Rimini*, *Imola*, *Meldola* and *Cesena*; Gelichi, in Brogiolo 1994, pp.160-61 and Gelichi, in Brogiolo 1996, p.70.

[85] It is significant that also in 7th-century *Pavia*, capital of the Longobard kingdom, the sewer system and road network were perfectly maintained (Brogiolo, in Randsborg 1989, p.157).

[86] The document dates back to 616-19, but it is not known whether the aforesaid banker had ever lived in the house concerned, a fact which could indicate a mid/high-status edifice; Gelichi, in Brogiolo 1994, pp.161-62.

[87] *Ib.*, pp.162-63. From the archaeological data the wooden house pattern emerges as characterised by its small size (due also to the common division of these structures beginning from the third century), sometimes with two storeys, more rarely with infrastructures of any style (*balnea*, cesspits), nearly always with a *portico* and shared courtyards and wells.

[88] At *Castelvecchio di Filattiera* (*Lunigiana*), during the Byzantine period, the defensive circuit and one or more towers were also made of wood, according to a sort of 'entrenched camp' enclosure technique that must have been certainly well known among people who lived near the borders of the Empire (the presence of foreign garrisons, possibly from regions beyond the Alps, has been put forward as plausible, also

In her study on *Verona*, La Rocca stresses the considerable stone-work activity, which should have also caused despoliation and the collection and trading of salvage, to be then recycled for new constructions in the 'most active' quarters (according to the patchwork planning so typical of Early Medieval towns), while perishable materials should have been generally used for annexes or secondary structures:[89] Certainly, there is the existence of a good level of building (*i.e.*, churches, ecclesiastical residences, etc.), notwithstanding the fact that the classical technical skills had sharply declined and only few features have survived (for example the *opus romanense* or *gallicum*), mostly performed by migratory workers as the demand (almost exclusively from the upper classes) grew less and less.[90]

Several reasons explain the position, generally being consequent on the social and economic changes that began as early as the 'Tetrarchic' period, which, in respect of building, brought to an end quarrying industries and brickworks on a broad scale by the 6th century (Arthur), and caused a reduction in building-production cycles, as is clearly shown by the loss (or disuse) of specialized handicrafts (such stone-cutting and dressing).[91]

Relating to the above, some consideration of Longobard customs and orders of the regions involved is relevant here. It has been particularly stressed that the Germanic upper classes were less affluent than the aristocracy of the Late Antique, or even the Merovingian and Carolingian periods. In short, there was not a ruling elite (immediately beneath the king and dukes) wealthy enough to promote the real-estate market; moreover, its interests and financial assets were normally used for funerary products (especially during the first period).[92]

In the light of this, the lack (or scarce evidence) of court and palace building is by no means surprising, and

prevents a complete archaeological analysis.[93] At *Monza* foundation walls were discovered that belonged to two apse-shaped halls, which, following Paul the Deacon, could refer to the residences ordered first by *Theodoric* and later by *Theodolind*, although the inaccurate excavation carried out cannot provide any further research survey. Nevertheless, to judge from their plans, they appear similar to Gothic examples (*i.e.*, *Monte Barro*), which had been affected by the Late Antique fortified *villa* pattern and will eventually also have represented a model for the Early Medieval architecture of the ruling classes.[94]

Similarly, there are few remaining details of the political and administrative centres (*curiae regis*, *ducis*) that reused Roman public buildings, which had sometimes even been rearranged previously (a well-known case is at *Brescia*, where there is a winged hall that had a colonnaded *portico* added in the Longobard period).[95] This practice is found in Byzantine areas as well, reflected in the material continuity of an authority directly inherited from the Western Empire.[96] At *Ravenna*, *Theodoric*'s Palace (perhaps to be dated back to the time of *Onorius*) was certainly the seat of exarchs and also of *Aistulf*, but the subsequent events that brought about its dramatic decay in Carolingian times are unknown. The same is true for the residence ordered by the *Ottos* and located outside *St. Lorenzo*'s Gate.[97] In Rome, the buildings on the *Palatine* were maintained at least until the end of the 7th century under the Byzantines (even though some nearby areas had fallen into decay from the 4th-5th centuries); nevertheless, after the short sojourn of the pontiffs, our knowledge of them fades away until after the erection of the Frangipane towers.[98]

By about the second half of the 7th century, the religious establishment (and its structures) must have drawn a great deal of interest as well as private funds. Nevertheless, considering the distribution of wealth of the Longobard economic system, the most remarkable buildings should rather be attributed to royal (or court) personages, who were actually allowed to manage the exchequers (clear examples are the *St. Salvatore* at *Brescia* and *St. Maria*

---

considering the multi-ethnic Byzantine armies); Cagnana, in Brogiolo 1994, p.172.

[89] La Rocca 1986, pp.64 and foll.

[90] Cagnana, in Gelichi (ed.) 1997, p.446. Regarding *Liguria*, the author notes a break around the middle of the 7th century, when the Longobard conquest brought to an end the building of urban schools, which had survived, although to a lesser extent, under the Byzantines. A striking consequence seems to have been the low-level standardization of techniques and styles common to most of the regions of central and northern Italy, including those of high-status, masonry constructions (for example, the disappearance of the *petit appareil* that had distinguished the western from the eastern districts of *Liguria*).

[91] Some explanatory examples: in *Liguria* the ending of quarrying activity by the 4th century (Mannoni; see note 90 above, Cagnana, p.446); no evidence, after the 3rd century, of any construction using large, squared stones (for *Liguria*; *ib.*), nor of any new brick production at *Lucca* (Castillo 2000, p.151). In addition, one should take into account the increased difficulties in transport, especially of heavy materials (Catarsi Dall'Aglio, in Brogiolo 1994, p.155). This eventually lead to the disappearance of *pozzolana* (volcanic ash and tuffa, typical building materials of *Latium*), as is proved by the 6th- and 7th-century works at *Portus Romae*; Coccia, in Paroli – Delogu 1993, p.193 and note 20.

[92] See also *infra* Chapter 1, note 42 and 50.

[93] Wickham (quoting from Balzaretti), in Francovich – Noyé 1994, p.741.

[94] Brogiolo 1994, pp.104-05. The palace at *Monte Barro*, made up of several buildings placed around a spacious courtyard, was a two-storey one, and the first floor was probably embellished with frescos (although quite rough) and a number of furnishings, especially the presumed audience halls (the finding of a hanging bronze crown would also indicate it as place of power).

[95] Brogiolo 1993, pp.58 and foll.

[96] The survival of some Late Antique edifices into the Early Middle Ages is mostly attested by literary sources. In the 9th century, *Agnellus* of *Ravenna* could still admire, in the Palaces of *Ravenna* and *Pavia*, the mosaics depicting *Theodoric sedentem super equum* (Agnellus, 333-34), while the Palace of *Verona* features in the so-called 'Bishop *Raterius* Picture', differently dated to the interval between the 8th and 10th century; Brogiolo 1994, p.105.

[97] Gelichi, in Brogiolo 1994, p.165.

[98] Ward Perkins 1984, p.167; Augenti, in Francovich – Noyé 1994, pp.686-87.

*foris portas* at *Castelseprio*).[99] Public monies were certainly also used for the large amounts of urban activity promoted by *Arechis II* at *Salerno*. And yet, in Carolingian times, the most considerable civil works of 9th- and 10th-century Rome, brought to light by survey, were probably due to the patronage of the aristocratic elite. There are no documentary sources about the houses of *Nerva*'s *Forum*, but, on the other hand, the improvements to *Trajan*'s *Forum* and the restoration of the residences placed there should have eventually been dependent on state intervention (someone has suggested *Albericus* or his followers).[100]

Archaeological finds attest to the use of tuffa and travertine stone (typical of the *Latium* region, in particular of the Roman context), and, in any case, show the great care given to these buildings, taking into account that the most urgent considerations of contractors of the 11th and 12th centuries would have been the availability and supply of raw materials; they would have relied as much as possible on local (and easy to work ) materials.[101] The difficulties which arose certainly resulted in the spoiling, recovery and re-use of materials and selection of more simple techniques and styles – such as wooden constructions.

However, these could even reach a high level (Mannoni) and, to this point, of note is the unexpected discovery of to a middle/upper-class wooden house found in the centre of 11th-/12th-century *Bologna* (what is more the later additions and rebuilding seem to have followed its original plan.[102]

Taking into account the high standards of technical quality attainable with wood (above all in Scandinavia), in Italy, where a strong stone tradition had become deep-rooted with the Romans, the widespread use of timber

would have reflected a significant departure in building styles, and it is not unreasonable to hold that some centres were still influenced, at least notionally, by the ancient building culture. An examples is the cathedral of *St. Giovanni* and *Reparata* at *Lucca*, where, in two of the most exacting works of the Early Medieval period, not only spoilt material was discarded, but, above all, the plaster was scratched to produce imitation *opus-quadratum* work, a technique lost until about the 12th century, by which time long production cycles, especially stone-cutting and dressing, had been introduced again.[103]

---

[99] See also *infra* Chapter 1, text and note 42.

[100] Meneghini 2000, p.303-foll. and Meneghini, in Brogiolo (ed.) 2000, pp.1-6. In the light of archaeological data, the *Forum* of *Trajan* was reclaimed around the middle of the 9th century (the ballasts consist of a great deal of pottery dating from the 1st millennium BC to the 6th century AD, whereas 1% can be referred to the 9th and 10th centuries). Nevertheless, it must have been demolished before the end of the 9th century (possibly consequent on a great and sudden demand for materials; *e.g.* the circuit of walls ordered by Pope *Leo IV*?) and modified again during the early decades of the 10th century. The ups and downs of such a public place may even mirror the eventual conflicts between the Pope and the unruly Roman aristocracy of the time (a hint in this sense in Marazzi, in Francovich – Noyé 1994, pp.650-52).

[101] In Tuscany, for instance, not earlier than the 11th or 12th century particular stones (such as *alberese*) came back into regular (high standard) use, instead of various sandstones that can be worked easily (Parenti, in Brogiolo 1994, p.32). The 'difficult' situation probably helped in the 'success' of *opus spicatum* (herringbone pattern) work too, throughout the Early Middle Ages (known even by Roman architects, as shown in the theatre of *Libarna*). This technique is attested, for example, at *Lomello*, where, however, bricks continued to be made until the 7th century (interesting in that even very small pieces were not discarded for building), and in *Genoa*, where the circuit of walls ordered by the bishop dates to the 10th century (the spoilt materials, nonetheless, appear to have been carefully reused, joined together and plastered with a lot of mortar); Cagnana, in Brogiolo 1994, pp.43-44.

[102] Gelichi, in Brogiolo 1994, p.165.

[103] Castillo 2000, p.153.

## 3. The coming of the 'Christian space'

### 3.1. The development of religious structures.

The Christianization of urban space certainly represents one of the fundamental elements that contributed to the setting up and shaping of the Early Medieval city, in particular through the rise of ecclesiastical sites, both cult and administrative, which progressively became important centralizing *foci*.[1]

By the 4th century a Christian topography had begun to emerge, which meant the decline, or, at least, fundamental changes to the previous planning (it consolidated over the next two centuries, achieving also an almost definitive map of the dioceses). Religious buildings encircled the ancient centres, making a sort of spiritual bulwark, more effective than the defensive walls themselves, although, according to the literary sources available, the new situation does not seem to have particularly impressed the contemporary writers. In the 6th century, Gregory of *Tours*, outlining the main urban characteristics, stressed the 'pagan decoration of the city-framework' (baths, theatre, *circus*), as being the only way of clearly distinguishing a town from other smaller or country contexts.[2]

The expansion of the Christian space, however, was rapid and, as early as the transition centuries between Late Antiquity and the Middle Ages, the foundations of the management system (that featured also the following ecclesiastical institutions) were firmly established.[3] Despite this, the phenomenon did not develop in a uniform way, in neither a chronological nor territorial respect, as would appear from Ambrose's policy or Constantine's imperial support, or from the favourable edicts (*i.e. Thessalonica*, AD 380).[4] Only few examples, in fact, usually coming from cities of a certain importance, took ready advantage of the possibilities offered by the situation post AD 313. In most contexts the establishment of a diocese, and, above all, buildings generally date from not earlier than the end of the 4th

century (with a complete definition occurring in the 5th and 6th centuries).[5] Certainly they depended on different social-economic factors (i.e. the extension and prosperity of communities), but political reasons may also have been a factor. For example, in the *Adriatic* area, where the Byzantines, while re-conquering and resettling the region during and after the Gothic War, made use of the episcopal office to raise to 'urban status' those centres specifically intended to control the territory.

Instead of displaying the vitality or wealth of the sites in question, the bishops' sees had therefore a strategic significance and provided those districts with new institutional strongholds.[6] In addition, most of the Roman *municipia* had joined the 'Three-Capitulars Schism', being later supported, in this sense, by the Aryan Longobards. (A prime example being *Cividale*, where, under the political privilege granted by *Julius Caesar*, the ruling factions and circuit walls manifested its urban identity.)[7]

Despite these observations, the religious features had been shaping the towns in a conclusive way by the later Empire Age, and fundamental aspects of interest are undoubtedly the ascertainment of the place and function of all those buildings that composed the ecclesiastical apparatus, *i.e.* burial and martyr-churches, monasteries, bishopric complexes, and, above all, the cathedral, which has always drawn particular attention. Scholars have dealt with this historiographic subject as far back as the 17th century, albeit the pioneer work, by Violante and Fonseca was only undertaken at the end of the 1960s. Although modified by recent researches, and also thanks to new archaeological findings, this study was clearly right in its analysis of our understanding of the meaning of

---

[1] Cantino Wataghin – Gurt Espaguerra – Guyon, in Brogiolo 1996, p.17.
[2] *Ib.*, p.36 (also for a reference to the source concerned: *Historia Francorum*, III, 19).
[3] The Greek-Gothic War, the Longobard Conquest as well as the transformation of some regions into frontier territory stood out among the causes of the shift of certain diocesan centres, although the general *scenario* does not appear as particularly disrupted. For example, the crisis of the religious system in *Abruzzi* can be cited, where the bishop's see moved away from *Aufinum*, *Castrum Truentinum* and *Sulmo* [Staffa, in Paroli 1997, pp.118-19]. Nevertheless, for certain districts, it must be taken into account that social and economical crises had begun in even earlier times (southern *Piedmont*, southern *Etruria*; see Chapter 2, notes 63, 64).
[4] Testini – Cantino Wataghin – Pani Ermini 1989, p.13.

[5] *Ib.*, p.13. It is worth noting that the widespread establishment of dioceses in central and southern Italy (during the second half of the 5th century) may be read as the response of the Church to particular events, such as the arrival of the Goths (although there is no clear evidence in this sense; *ib.*, p.58). Yet, in the light of literary sources, the raising of *Montefeltro* to the status of diocese may also be seen as a sort of claim, nonetheless as also an important means of evangelization, after the Longobard conquest of the region that occurred in the first two decades of the 7th century; Bernacchia, in Paroli 1997, p.12.
[6] La Rocca, in Francovich – Noyé 1994, p.551. To judge from the available excavation data, the religious buildings seem to have been the only ones to balance the customary poverty of the centres (*Concordia*, *Eraclea*). The erection of ecclesiastical complexes had there a political meaning too, with propagandist intent, as emerges from certain dedicatory inscriptions which definitely disparage the poverty of the previous edifices (Wataghin, in Brogiolo 1996, p.36).
[7] It is significant that the move of the bishop of *Zuglio* to *Cividale* made the patriarch of *Aquileia* envious. The latter was forced to live at *Cormons* '*tantum vulgo sociatus*', while the former resided where the duke and the Germanic elite did. In Longobard contexts, the presence of the ruling classes seems to have resulted in the community being called a real town (La Rocca, in Francovich – Noyé 1994, p.552 and note 29).

'cathedral', a controversial concept over the centuries and not properly defined until the Late Middle Ages.[8]

This should indeed be taken into account, especially for those situations where either the site or functions of the *ecclesia mater* seem to be free from the usual standards. Certain models tended to be quite common within the peninsular regions as a whole, beyond the obvious and natural local differences. On the other hand, an exact categorization cannot be arrived at, since the patterns of settlement, as well as the solutions chosen, were not really within a limited range, and also because of the limitations of the field-survey itself. Apart from the lack of thorough recordings (although the data is not insignificant), one must admit the difficulty for the research to materially distinguish the bishop's church from any other Christian religious building.[9]

Nevertheless, as also emerged from the *XI Congrès International d'Archèologie Chrètienne*, the archaeological contribution is of considerable importance, insomuch as the 'traditional' positions regarding to the cathedral and its relevant problems (based almost exclusively on studies of the documentary sources) have been put back into perspective. On the other hand, new approaches have developed, achieving more thorough results and creating an essential research framework for future data.[10]

One major result, for most scholars, is the abandonment of the former hypothesis in relation to the old *topos*, which maintained that the cathedral was generally situated in the suburbs, beyond the limits of the circuit walls, in cemetery areas, and usually commissioned by the first bishop – who will have found there his eternal repose.

Ambrose himself was buried elsewhere, in the *basilica martyrum* (and another striking example is the case of *Brescia*[11]), whilst the building of the *ecclesia* undertaken by him would rather attest, as previously mentioned, to exceptional circumstances relevant to the most important cities, where certain possibilities of the kind were immediately allowed.

Conversely, the archaeological data gathered hitherto often bears witness to a significant gap between the earliest date referring to a given diocese and the erection of the bishop's church concerned – this having occurred not only for financial reasons, but as a result of the availability of a location suitable for cathedral's demands. Its duties, in fact, were initially limited within the specific cultic activity (christenings, celebration of mass, etc.) but they rapidly evolved, while its influence and scope increased (day-to-day administration, poor relief, officiating at funeral rites, *etc.*), eventually becoming symbolic of the religious and social community it served. Such developments entailed at times an 'imposing' construction, the growth of the episcopal complex (residences, various facilities, guesthouses, workshops, *etc.*), as well as an urban ecclesiastical network as a whole.[12]

Consequently, one ought not to expect the complex to be placed modestly away from the centre, but rather in a prominent position, certainly in a topographical sense, yet at the same time respecting the 'privileged state between the *ecclesia* and the built-up area'.[13] In terms of research, archaeology can eventually be the best way of investigation, first by checking the relationship with the city walls, which, in most cases, seem to enclose the bishop's church. Instead of the Republican era circuits, the Late Antiquity boundaries should rather be considered, as more accurate indicators of planning expansion and changes, so that a clearer picture may be had of the 'vitality' of the cathedral quarter.[14]

---

[8] Brogiolo – Gelichi 1998, pp.95-97 (also for a reference to Violante – Fonseca 1969). Attention can be drawn here to the problem of the so-called 'double cathedral' (among the best-known cases are Milan, *Brescia, Aquileia* and *Parenzo*).The bishop could obviously officiate at more than one place, especially on the occasion of particular feasts (even at burial churches), but the sole liturgical engagements do not provide the full explanation. On the other hand, in some cities, the presence of two episcopal churches at the same time could mean that the most suitable site for a monumental undertaking had not been available at the moment it was decided to erect it (actually the later edifice is always more refined in respect of both magnitude and care of construction. In spite of this, the problem has no easy solution, since at *Aquileia* the two 'cathedrals' may have been planned by the same project); Testini *et alii* 1989, pp.51-52).
[9] Brogiolo – Gelichi 1998, p.97. The baptistery as independent edifice (located at some distance from the bishop's church) may be a distinguishing element in central and southern Italy, helping to recognize the episcopal centre (an example could be from Florence, considering that the complex probably dates back to early Christian times). On the contrary, as regards the northern regions of the peninsula, any assertion of the kind would not seem really exact (at *Aosta* it is even placed inside the *ecclesia*, although the particular position upon the *forum* may eventually account for a limited space available); Testini *et alii* 1989, pp.62-63.
[10] Testini *et alii* 1989.

[11] In the light of literary sources it can be assumed that the early bishops of that Lombard city were inhumed in different burial churches (in accordance with the law, they were presumably the only buildings with such a function, at least up to a certain time); Brogiolo, in Paroli 1997, p.413.
[12] Wataghin, in Brogiolo 1996, p.27.
[13] *Ib.*, p.20.
[14] As regards the relationship between cathedral and city walls, the space-to-time ratio is difficult to fully understand in quite a few cases. At Florence (where parts of the circuit were demolished, as shown by Maetzke) the *foris muros* location of the cathedral, mentioned by some writers, could just indicate a general topographical reference (Testini 1989, p.77), but other situations appear more complicated. At *Pisa*, the *extra moenia* position may have also been consequent on lack of space inside the town, while, at *Arezzo* (about which it should be anyway stressed in terms of the ambiguous term of bishop's church), the specific military role of the fortress could have prevented any other 'civic' structures from taking place upon this (a reference is Citter, in Paroli 1997, p.207). The location of the cathedral of *Modena* (placed outside the walls in a cemetery area) may be evidence of the shift of the religious complex concerned, as well as of the town itself that occurred during the transition centuries (a direct cause could have been the well-known instability of the hydro-geological conditions typical of that region); Testini 1989, p.31 (who quotes from Gelichi).

The examples of *Aosta* and *Trieste* (where the *ecclesia* are closely connected to the *forum*) would therefore not appear more striking than other sites, where the 'strategic' position is denoted either by a close connection with the suburb (Milan, *Aquileia*, Rome itself), or by the nearness to important roads (Florence and Naples), or by its 'gravitation' around flourishing economic districts (*Ravenna*; *Luni*, fig.20).[15]

Nevertheless, the occupancy of certain public areas (however much of the original function they may have lost, they must anyhow have maintained an extremely imposing presence) could actually have been due to a privileged relationship between the bishop and the community, or, what is more, the civil authorities. At *Aosta* a special link with the clergy of Milan has been noted; in addition, political reasons might also have been behind some building solutions).[16]

Apart from these impressive cases, wherever the excavations have been thorough, the location of the bishop's church is attested to in areas that were anything but marginal.[17] Moreover, the available data indicates the probable uninterrupted use of the edifice chosen (either residential, or public, or more rarely religious), which would have changed its previous function for the new conditions.[18]

If such a *modus operandi* appears to reflect a certain practicality (to be viewed as part of a custom of re-use, fairly widespread from Late Antiquity onwards),[19] or

somewhat provisional solutions, possibly waiting at times before taking possession of areas more suitable for a monumental building. However, it must be emphasised that even the earliest planning was not characterized by any inaccurate or rushed work, since, in several cases, the medieval cathedral is recorded as still being on the site of original early Christian edifice.[20] Nevertheless, there are examples of relocation during the first phases of the Early Middle Ages, for both cult-edifice and episcopal see, caused by imminent dangers, and also crises of other kinds, which had generally begun some time back (before AD 595, the bishop's see moved to *Tuscania* from *Tarquinia*, where the proximity of the frontier, on the River *Mignone*, had dramatically affected a situation already long in decline: *cf.* Chapter I, note 79). Besides the famous instance of Milan, security reasons resulted in relocations elsewhere, *i.e.* at *Velletri* (decided by Pope Gregory the Great) and at *Ascoli*, where a site on an eminence, although within the town boundaries, replaced St Mary's Cathedral (not in use from the end of the 6th century to 745: archaeological surveys have found there layers with traces of destruction, dating back to the first phase of the Longobard invasion). The wide extension of such a phenomenon cannot really be asserted, and, furthermore, the flights of bishops in the northern *Adriatic* district (as mentioned in several written sources) could simply mean the renouncement of heresy, as concerns those Byzantine centres that will have then found in *Grado* a new institutional reference point.[21]

The practice of re-using various structures was, in that context, probably only partial, since most of the former constructions had to be largely redesigned to meet the requirements of the Christian liturgy (quite removed from the ancient pagan cult),[22] a fact that should be seen as

---

[15] In Milan it strategically settled in between the old political nucleus and the area developed throughout the early/mid-Imperial Age (where the Baths of *Maximian* were also built). In a largely exploited district, enclosed by the Late Antique circuit, the Cathedral of *Aquileia* was built, while in Rome it seems rather to have a close connection with the ancient *suburbium* (Testini 1989, pp.36, 40 and 17). In *Ravenna* and *Luni* it is situated near the port (of *Classe* in the former case; *ib.*, p.37). In Florence the two edifices contending for the role of the bishop's church were erected along the *Cassia* Way (*St. Reparata*, *St. Lorenzo*; Gelichi 1999, pp.66-67).

[16] In Milan, the cathedral seems to have linked the private and public quarters, as it was situated in between (Testini 1989, p.45). It is worth recalling, however, that *Theodosius* and Ambrose were bound by a special 'friendship' (the emperor formally submitted to the religious leader). The occupancy of state space by Christian institutions represents an interesting problem. In *Aquileia*, for example, it has to be wondered why the bishop and the religious community had the buildings of public *horrea* at their disposal (after their transfer), when they decided to erect the cult complex (*ib.*, pp.43-44).

[17] Among the best-known sites, it is only in *Turin* that the religious complex seems to have been built in an area not settled before. This finding may have been caused by limited surveys, nevertheless, one should not always try to apply a general fixed pattern to any situation (see Brogiolo – Gelichi 1998, pp.95-97). Alternatively, the cathedral of *Zuglio* was built in an unoccupied zone, but it was exactly located along an important road which, starting from the *forum*, connected *Aquileia* with the Alpine regions (Testini 1989, p.41).

[18] Wataghin, in Brogiolo 1996, p.35. However, it must be emphasised that verification is sometimes difficult (if not a complete 'catch 22' situation, when there are no stratigraphical data).

[19] *Ib.*, p.35. Some examples from Tuscany are explanatory. In Florence, the bishop's residence (4th to 5th century) was built upon *thermae* (still working until the 4th century), while at *Roselle*, the *ecclesia mater* (end of the 5th to early 6th century) took place in the baths of *Adrian*'s time

(certainly to exploit the piping system for christening activities as well); Gelichi 1999, pp.64 and 110. Such a solution has been found also in Rome, where a font was installed over a 3rd-century *domus*, which in turn had been built on baths dating to the 2nd century AD (Testini 1989, p.15). Worthy of remark is the case of the cathedral of *Chiusi*: its T-shaped apse seems to have been consequent on the previous reused structures, whereas the same pattern chosen for the church of *Roselle* might rather be ascribed to the influence of that on the latter town (Ciampoltrini 2002, p.441).

[20] Testini 1989, p.61. Archaeology can provide essential data for the persistence of a given building in a certain place, and possibly even its eventual role: for instance, during excavations at *St. Maria del Fiore* (Florence), some structures, probably of a *solea*, have been exposed (*ib.*, pp.61-62 and note 77), so that some scholars presume it to have been the bishop's church since early-Christian times. Conversely, in *Ancona*, the Church of *St. Lorenzo*, beneath the Medieval *St. Ciriaco*'s, does not seem to have had such a function (*ib.*, p.63). an extra-urban edifice near *Roselle* (located on the *Poggio Mosconcino*) was proposed as a cathedral, but the idea became unlikely as soon as archaeologists proved the lack of any pre-Romanesque phases; Gelichi 1999, p.112.

[21] La Rocca, in Francovich – Noyé 1994, p.551; about *Velletri* (Testini 1989, p.65, note 93); for *Ascoli*, Cappelli, in Paroli 1997, pp.86-87.

[22] Wataghin, in Brogiolo 1996, p.35. Gelichi 1999, p.64 (and note 34 for Cardini's suggestion). It is important to ascertain the gradual increase of Church property and assets. While the bishop of *Ascoli* must have been quite 'wealthy', considering that he paid the Longobards to ransom his fellow citizens, the *scenario* of 6th-7th century Rome appears impressive in the light of certain results. The ecclesiastical institutions would have owned (or, at least, exploited) the Baths of *Caracalla*, of

THE HISTORY OF EARLY MEDIEVAL TOWN OF NORTH AND CENTRAL ITALY: THE CONTRIBUTION OF ARCHAEOLOGICAL EVIDENCE

crucial in terms of the funding and planning problems of such an undertaking, not depending solely on ecclesiastical decisions. This must have been true at least until well into the 5th century, when Church assets had finally reached a critical mass. An interesting example can be found in Florence, where the present *Piazza St. Giovanni* area was progressively acquired by the ecclesiastical institutions between the 4th and 5th centuries. Developed as the heart of a new religious centre, the complex has even been supposed to have been erected in one phase, although such an hypothesis is only backed by an historical-architectural study; fig.21).[23]

Before the days of *Theodosius* there was no wholesale conversion to Christianity of the aristocratic classes, whose interests and donations (in addition to the rest of the community) would certainly have been fundamental to the developing cult. It is noteworthy that within certain contexts either the authority or prestige of the bishop could exert some pressure, if not enforce decisions in this regard.[24] The accomplishment of the cathedral project, in fact, was usually dependent on the financial efforts of both clergy and congregation, whereas imperial support does not seem to have continued after Constantine, as the position in Milan seems to confirm. Regarding the *basilica nova*, some state influence has been suggested, but a large community (and one close to the court), could well explain the imposing scale of the undertaking as well as its parallels with the public architecture of the time.[25]

The religious backdrop was finally completed by other buildings, to be partially considered as subsidiary, as well as sharing with the *ecclesia mater* the liturgical and organizational functions expected.[26] Examples of these complexes included monasteries, burial and martyr/*ad sanctos* churches, and (with different degrees of importance depending on the specific urban context) general parish as well as edifices for worship (these latter were often erected by private individuals and clearly displayed their interest and scope, either spiritually, socially or symbolically).[27]

Among those types of buildings there are some early examples (in Rome and Milan, once again promoted by Constantine and/or the episcopal activity of Ambrose), although it was in the 5th and 6th centuries that the framework of Christian topography set about consolidating,[28] in particular, also, within the suburbs, where, replacing sometimes more modest shrines, new edifices were set up (the architectural style of which appears to have been influenced to a certain extent by the *Po*-Valley model over quite a wide geographical area, as with *St. Vincenzo* at *Lucca*).[29]

Burial- and martyr-churches (their roles overlapped quite early) show archaeological evidence of some consequence, since their either 'cross or oval-shaped' patterns (for cultic reasons also) represent a fairly typical and distinctive element compared to the canonical *basilica* lay-out.[30] In addition, as far as purposes here are concerned, it is worth stressing the impact they had on the extra-urban territory, where they were located because of their function – mainly funeral (according to the laws in force).

Outside the towns, the Roman landscape consisted of a great variety of productive activities, workshops, residential houses, and *necropolises*, set along the roads. The buildings in question were erected over these foundations, occupying areas already reserved for

---

*Decius*, perhaps those of *Diocletian* and of Constantine, as well as other areas, such as the *Porticus Minucia*, that of *Livia, etc.* (Meneghini – Santangeli Valenzani 1995, p.287).

[23] Gelichi 1999, p.64 (and note 34 for Cardini's suggestion). It is important to ascertain the gradual increase of Church property and assets. While the bishop of *Ascoli* must have been quite 'wealthy', considering that he paid the Longobards to ransom his fellow citizens, the *scenario* of 6th-7th century Rome appears impressive in the light of certain results. The ecclesiastical institutions would have owned (or, at least, exploited) the Baths of *Caracalla*, of *Decius*, perhaps those of *Diocletian* and of Constantine, as well as other areas, such as the *Porticus Minucia*, that of *Livia, etc.* (Meneghini – Santangeli Valenzani 1995, p.287).

[24] Wataghin, in Brogiolo 1996, p.36; the author reports a significant source relevant to the French town of *Auxerre*, where the bishop put pressure on a certain *Stefanus Africanus* to take possession of a plot more suitable to the great newly-planned cathedral (necessary to meet the increase in size of the religious community). It is important to remark here that an earlier chronology should not be discarded as regards ecclesiastical organization and structures of some consequence, as would emerge from several studies carried out by scholars especially in Spain, South France and *Dalmatia* (certain situations would date back to the first decades of the 4th century). Among others, some specific references could be Chevalier 1995, Godoy Fernandez 1989, Ripoll – Velazquez 1999, Saxer 1999, Bratoz 1999. I am very grateful to my colleague and friend Dr Stefano Roascio, who has drawn my attention to this problem. Moreover, we both work on an excavation and research project at *Illegio* (*Udine*, North-Eastern Italy), led by Dr Aurora Cagnana, where the first phases of *St. Paolo*'s Church can unexpectedly be ascribed to a very early Christian date (c. AD 337-441, by carbon-14 dating). In addition, this is well in accordance with the resolution of the Council of *Aquileia* (AD 380), who tried to promote widespread evangelization and establish a definite planning structure over both rural and mountainous areas. (Cagnana – Roascio, in Francovich [ed.] 2006, pp.304-10).

[25] Testini 1989, pp.43-44 (and note 45).

[26] Wataghin, in Brogiolo 1996, pp.20, 23.

[27] As the archaeological data emphasizes, the poverty of house architecture (see also note 6 *infra*) is often in contrast with the considerable building styles and activities that characterize the religious complexes; this can also be seen in the light of the special relationship, consolidated throughout the Longobard and Carolingian eras, between the aristocracy and ecclesiastical elite. An example might be the stone inscription from Tuscany (first quarter of the 8th century) that attests to the foundation of two churches (*St. Giusto* and *St. Clemente*), perhaps by *gastaldus Alchis* (Gelichi 1999, p.80). It must also be stressed that, in the late 7th-century *Maremma* Region, it was the investment in religious buildings (and not in grave goods) that indicates the status of the ruling classes in *Lucca* or *Chiusi* (Citter, in Paroli 1997, p.203).

[28] In that period, in fact, the expansion of Christianization also entailed the erection of cult buildings in small centres – wherever religious communities were managed by an established clergy (Wataghin, in Brogiolo 1996, pp.29-30). Among early examples, apart from a couple of edifices from Florence, the cult hall beneath the ancient Church of *St. Martino* at *Padua* can be mentioned (*ib.*, p.23).

[29] Archaeology confirms the pattern of the church of *Lucca* (5th century): cross-shaped plan, square transept and semicircular apse; Gelichi 1999, p.28.

[30] Brogiolo – Gelichi 1998, pp. 97-98.

cemeteries and (subsequently) also developing new ones, without necessarily abandoning any complex not related to this practice.[31]

From certain sources of later centuries (or indeed of the Late Middle Ages) it emerges that some of those cult sites even contended with the *ecclesia mater* for the title of 'cathedral', going at times so far as to claim the bishop's see (with success in the well-known case of *Vercelli*).[32]

Let us assert once more the loose concept of 'episcopal church' throughout the Early Medieval period and assume, as well, that the bishop could officiate at the same time, eventually at special ceremonies, at burial churches too (possibly connected to a particular memory). On the other hand, taking obviously into account likely favourable economic circumstances in the surrounding regions, it should be noted that as several cult/martyr complexes represented a strong attraction not only for grave sites, or even housing areas, but also for pilgrims, this entailed a large amount of planning and management, as well as facilities (reception, welfare and relief structures and services). Instances of shift from the ancient urban centres were indeed not infrequent, as the striking example of *Ostia* shows. *Gregoriopolis* rose up in the 9th century over a built-up area originally settled close to, and surrounding, the *basilica* as well as the cemetery where the martyrs *Cryse* and Saint *Monica* lay. The old town instead became curiously a burial space and, in order to reach *St. Ciriaco*'s Church there, a certain presbyter *Andrea* had to go, in 1162, via a path 'with many bushes, cat's-backs and graves', presumably the old *decumanus maximus*.[33] Some tombs soon stood out among the others placed on the same site, because of the fame of either a bishop, martyr or saint buried there, and thus during the later growth of his cult, once the mortal remains had been transferred, would have been guarded by the nearby monastery.[34]

There are a number of resulting interesting research problems connected with the latter, as their foundations were often affected by actual socio-economic factors, after they had had a previous phase of 'ephemeral' community life experiences which, although attested to since the 4th century, left scant material evidence. In this respect, some structures connected with the episcopal complexes at *Vercelli* and *Aquileia* could be mentioned, while the French case of *Marmoutier* would indicate that even the oldest coenobitic forms are not necessarily to be sought close to, nor within the spatial scope, of the *ecclesia mater*).[35] In some regions beyond the Alps, the development of monasteries began as early as the Merovingian era (there is a famous example at *Poitiers*, commissioned in 540 by *Radegonde, Chlotar*'s wife).[36] On the contrary, with regard to the Italian peninsula, remains of some importance date only from the Longobard and Carolingian Age, when these institutions improved and consolidated, representing then also a way of strengthening family estates, nonetheless, becoming a consequent means of territorial control in the hands of the aristocracy.[37]

It has already been highlighted elsewhere[38] that the monasteries may have played a positive role in the economic recovery of towns, and, in particular, their interaction with/within the production system of the very Early Middle Ages, if it were indeed the case that those institutions had already achieved a defined and stable organizational level at that time. An idea of this is certainly well backed up by the unexpected data from *Crypta Balbi*, nonetheless, even a less prominent context (such as at *Ascoli*) would likewise indicate that the monastic communities had a remarkable role in the local urban economy, in this case, mostly farming (concomitant too with the slow institutional restoration that occurred from the time of Bishop *Auderis*, 745-80).[39] Additionally, in the light of some evidence from the Tuscany region, the interesting connection between monasteries and mining activity can be assumed, what is more, often relevant to demesne areas.[40]

A conclusive factor should be the possible relationship that these religious complexes may have had with the civil leadership, as has been hypothesised on the basis of some archaeological finds (at least suggestive, although more difficult to ascertain than the written sources). The building planning of them does not seem to have taken over an eventual pattern before the second half the 8th century (*e.g. Novalesa* Abbey), so that certain

[31] Wataghin, in Brogiolo 1996, p.33.
[32] Testini 1989, p.29. The archaeological analysis often presents real difficulties in terms of ascertaining the specific role of a given building (see *infra* note 9), since even 'minor' churches were then provided with a baptismal font (for the religious community nearby). Moreover, because of the dramatic lack of written sources before the middle of the Early Medieval era, it is hard to check any supposed shift of the bishop's hall during the early Christian period (especially when all traces and memory of it have faded away: a striking example is from *Modena*, as only late written sources tell of the Martyr Church of *St. Giminiano*, referred to as an episcopal church); Wataghin, in Brogiolo 1996, p.32.
[33] Fasola – Fiocchi Nicolai, 1989, pp.1203-05. Rome, the most famous cult place, well shows the huge organization the pilgrimage industry entailed (although that city led the way in this). As well as lodges and residences, there were also libraries, schools, hospices, baths, *etc.* (*ib.*, p.1197).
[34] Wataghin, in Brogiolo 1996, p.27. It is worth noting that it could also be the case for tombs of important lay people, as well as kings and the nobility (in particular of Longobard Age); Lusuardi Siena – Giostra – Spalla, in Brogiolo 2000.

[35] Wataghin, in Brogiolo 1996, pp.30, 26.
[36] Lusuardi Siena *et alii*, in Brogiolo 2000, pp.275 and foll.
[37] About this topic, *cf.* especially La Rocca, in Paroli 1997.
[38] See Chapter 1, final remarks and, in particular, references to Balzaretti, in Christie – Loseby 1996.
[39] Cappelli, in Paroli 1997, pp.88-89.
[40] Citter, in Brogiolo – Wataghin 1998, p.189: the author stresses the significant parallels with Germany (*ib.*, note 77); it must be said that the possession of woodlands and watercourses (as sometimes emerges from literary sources) may reveal such activities.

construction solutions ought to be simply regarded as 'experiments', in order to find a proper and more defined structural typology. Nevertheless, in the first phase of *St. Salvatore* at *Brescia*, the halls, disposed orthogonally around a courtyard, would recall audience buildings of previous times and, as they would be unlikely to match any monastic function, may reveal a secular duty within the scope of the nearby royal palace.[41] Further to this, it is appropriate to mention and estimate the utilization of pre-existent towers. Linked to the widespread phenomenon of re-using ancient structures, common also for monasteries, the towers may also represent early examples (well before the 10th century) of tower-houses, intended as 'architecture of power' (Settia).[42]

## 3.2. Custom and regulation upon burials.

Roman laws decreed clearly that space for the dead had to be located outside the city walls, either for health or reasons of *decorum*, and, since these restrictions were usually observed, the *necropolises* were often set along the main extra-urban roads.[43]

Such cemeteries, according also to a general phenomenon of structural and material re-use, typical of Late Antiquity and the Early Middle Ages, became at the same time the last abode of Christians too, who, rearranging them in order to meet their needs (more space required because of exclusive inhumations), actually showed a certain practicality, often sharing the site with pagan burials, even though they were kept clearly segregated (a fact scarcely accepted by past historians, unless regarding the very early period).[44]

By the 4th century, the churches were erected upon funerary areas, and especially their *basilicas* became at the same time both an element of regulation (dictating the orientations of graves towards the tomb of the martyr) and disruption of the ancient planning systems (since even the presence of the *mausoleums* of illustrious men and women could not be comparable to that extent).[45]

As mentioned above, some of those sites were to become remarkable religious centres, often ruled over by monasteries, as well as large built-up areas – at times real autonomous villages[46] – while suburban cemeteries generally continued to be used until the 8th century,[47]

although the *scenario* was very variable, mostly depending on the *status quo* of the times and diverse contexts. Related to this, apart from special worshipped martyr sites,[48] one should mention the importance of a given site also in previous times, possibly as consequent on its nearness to certain principal roads (*Aosta*; fig.22.)[49] In addition there were also other factors, such as the custom of burying in a specific area dating from prehistoric times, the shift of town centres, the construction of defensive walls, or the presence of a garrison.[50]

The Longobards themselves exploited the ancient cemeteries outside the city boundaries, but over the last hundred years or so of their reign a change clearly began to occur, which, by the 8th century, saw burials brought to urban churchyards, under a new rising form of order.[51] It was a slow and certainly not a one-way process, and one to be viewed as ensuing from a progressive approach to the space afforded to the dead, while the study of its relationship with the post-Republican walls would seem to be very profitable, insofar as some results might be quite unexpected (as with the case of *Cividale*).[52]

When and how previous gravesites began being used by cities is still a controversial question. An exact chronology is difficult to produce, while, on the other hand, research has provided new data that permits the zones in question in part to move out of the old *topos* of neglect.[53] Certainly one should not underrate – if not as the sole cause, at least as a contributing factor – the endless cycles of warfare: from the early barbarian invasions, through the Greek/Gothic conflicts, up to the coming of the Longobards. Some situations from the *Abruzzi* region appear very serious; in Rome, the great burial grounds (*i.e. St. Eusebius* on the *Esquiline* Hill) only developed after the long siege by *Witiges* in 537-38.[54] Nevertheless, a change in mentality should also be

---

[41] Wataghin, in Gelichi (ed.) 1997, p.266 and foll.
[42] Quoted *ib.*, p.267.
[43] Brogiolo – Gelichi 1998, p.98.
[44] Fasola – Fiocchi Nicolai 1989, pp.1154-57 (who cite some examples from Rome). Practical choices can also be assumed about the location of certain burials (actually not that close to town), possibly due to the availability of plots eventually given by benefactors (*ib.*, p.1156).
[45] *Ib.*, pp.1175, 1178.
[46] See *infra* note 33.
[47] Brogiolo – Wataghin 1998, p.230.

[48] The burials of the early bishops of *Brescia* too (placed in the Churches of *St. Alessandro, St. Faustino ad sanguinem*) would indicate different solutions (not conforming to any regulations fixed in advance); Brogiolo, in Paroli 1997, p.413.
[49] Perinetti 1989, pp.1217 and foll.
[50] At *Arezzo*, in the suburb called *St. Croce*, a Longobard *necropolis*, interestingly not connected with any church, has been related to the military presence on the *Arx* (stronghold); Citter, in Paroli 1997, p.207.
[51] Brogiolo – Gelichi 1998, p.101. This did not necessarily imply an utter desertion of suburban *necropoles* (at *Aosta*, one was used until modern times; Brogiolo – Wataghin 1998, p.230). Interesting is the case of *Lucca*, where barely one tomb has been counted outside the circle of walls (Church of *St. Frediano*); Degasperi 1995, pp.541 and foll.
[52] If its relationship with the boundary walls were confirmed, one *necropolis* would have been *intra moenia* as early as mid-Imperial times (Brogiolo – Wataghin 1998, p.230). However, it was actually from the 3rd-4th centuries that a certain tendency of locating burials near the town began to take place (Wataghin – Lambert, *ib.*, p.103).
[53] Brogiolo – Gelichi 1998, p.100.
[54] For *Abruzzi*, Staffa, in Paroli 1997, p.117 and foll.; as Osborne asserts, the Greek/Gothic War must have been one of the main causes of *intra moenia* burials, nonetheless, it should be remembered at the same time that the extra-urban *necropolises* of Rome were restored up to the 6th and 7th century (Meneghini – Santangeli, in Paroli – Delogu 1993, pp.92-93 and note 34.

looked for (possibly influenced by the Christian ideology), while economic variables must have probably played a consequent role at the same time (the carrying of the corpse to a distant site, with new and old ritual ceremonies, may have reasonably represented quite an exacting charge for a society less wealthy than the Roman one).[55]

Archaeological evidence indicates the widespread and well-defined practice of inhumations *in urbe* in the course of the 6th century. Despite this, even if finds are rare for the 5th century, and almost exceptional for the 4th, by no means is there a need to refer them necessarily to situations of danger or emergency, nor regard them as free from any sort of regulation, however precocious they may have been.

In her article on *Verona*, La Rocca pointed out that most of the graves were placed in the eastern part of the town, strictly linked (what is more) to demesne lands (in contrast to the western one, rather marked by residential quarters), indicating thus an organization of some kind (if not real regulations).[56] Judging from the current knowledge and data, this interesting prospect does not match a largely extendible pattern, considering that at *Lucca*, for instance, the selected areas seem to have been generally private; on the other hand, isolated tombs may possibly just mean the presence of a cult building in the past, traces of which have never been found by survey.[57] Such an analytical approach might be essential, in particular, with respect to the study of that practice of land transfer, from state to private properties (in order to maintain an urban *decorum* or to prevent old buildings from falling into disrepair),[58] as well as of the role the Church may have had, since early times, in the management of some plots and in the organization of burial matters within the scope of a given town.

Concerning this, certain evidence is noteworthy, specifically coming from the Italian capital. Archaeology has indicated that in several cases graves lay inside

enclosed structures, such as baths and warehouses (at *Portus Romae*).[59] Thus they were well-defined spaces, which truly reflected the Christian concept of a place of eternal repose, of a 'dormitory for the brothers'.[60] In addition, in spite of the dramatic paucity of field matches, some imperial confiscations and restitutions would prove that, as early as AD 257, the ecclesiastical institution owned properties within and beyond the city boundaries, nonetheless having a hand in ruling over cemeteries, at the time when "burials were no longer a private or family business but part of the community as a whole".[61]

Such evidence would definitely suggest a consolidation of Church assets, which will have further increased and strengthened in the course of the 5th century, offering in the end, as mentioned before, quite an imposing *scenario*, if the picture of 6th-/7th-century Rome is to be relied upon.[62] Other relevant tokens – if not of direct possession, at least with the ability to exploit some public areas and ancient edifices – could be revealed through an accurate investigation of commercial transactions, regarding both the material used for graves (*i.e.* (spoilt) (head)stones with inscriptions) and, above all, the sale of burial niches. On this matter, literary sources attest repeatedly to such activities handled by *praepositi* or presbyters, and pertaining to cult buildings (as some documents of the years 521-25 do), whereas a funerary epigraph would presuppose businesses of this kind for the area upon the *Coliseum* also, apparently far from any religious structure (but probably within the clerical scope, as there is no evidence of any civil administration in this sense).[63]

The ecclesiastical institution, however, had a conclusive part in causing the practice of out-of-town burials being abandoned, specifically by means of urban churches and, in particular, in the 5th and 6th centuries, before the parish system had been established, with the cathedrals indeed.[64]

A detailed perspective on the ways such a phenomenon developed cannot be easily reached, having also to consider that they often escaped the religious authority's

---

[55] *Ib.*, p.93. An interesting point is that the decrease in the number and quality of tableware types, as emerges from 5th/6th century grave-goods, may also mirror the trade 'crisis' stressed elsewhere (Gastaldo, in Brogiolo – Wataghin 1998, p.31). Wataghin, on the other hand, points out a different cultural approach (actually some *necropolises*, fairly distant from the town, show quite a protracted use, in spite of the existence of other sites closer to the centre (in Brogiolo – Wataghin 1998, p.103).

[56] La Rocca 1986, pp.39 and foll.; also Brogiolo – Gelichi 1998, pp.98-99, especially for some remarks dealt with further.

[57] Significant is the case of some burials near the Baths of *Diocletian*: they do not really show any evident connection with that building, whereas they could be related to the Church of *St. Ciriaco in Thermis* (known by literary sources), to which a number of marble decorative fragments found nearby could perhaps be attributed (Meneghini – Santangeli 1995, p.283). About *Lucca*, Degasperi 1995, pp.541-foll. The case of *Amiternum* can be mentioned here as well. The tombs located in the vicinity of the amphitheatre can be explained by the presence of the nearby cathedral, whilst those placed in the area of the theatre do not seem to have fallen within the ambit of any religious institution. Nevertheless their arrangement appears to be out of any exact rule (Giuntella, in Brogiolo – Wataghin 1998, p.62).

[58] See Chapter 2, note 68.

[59] Coccia, in Paroli – Delogu 1993, p.184.

[60] Fasola – Fiocchi Nicolai 1989, p.1170.

[61] *Ib.*, p.1192, note 131, where the analysis starts from the situation of Rome. On the other hand in Milan the excavation data from the site of the *Cattolica* University would indicate that a certain cemetery had been managed privately (still during and after Ambrose's episcopacy); moreover, it seems to have been commonly used simultaneously by both Christians and pagans (Wataghin – Lambert, in Brogiolo – Wataghin 1998, p.105).

[62] See note 23 above.

[63] *Ib.*, pp.286 and foll.; the inscription tells of a burial niche purchased by a couple for their daughter, indicating activity of this kind in the quarter near the Amphitheatre, which had lost its original function and was being used as a quarry.

[64] Brogiolo – Gelichi 1998, p.100. It is noteworthy that none of them is before the second half of the 6th century, whereas late-Imperial (*Theodosian*-Age) laws warned only against tombs encumbering roads and urban public spaces (Lambert, in Paroli 1997, p.288, note 21 and p.287).

control, as would rather seem to emerge from some canonical prescriptions. If the councils dealing with this question just confirmed at first the prohibition of inhuming inside churches and baptisteries (*Braga*, AD 563; *Mâcon*, 585; *Nantes*, 658?, *etc.*),[65] later, that of *Mainz* (at the beginning of the 9th century) allowed clergymen and nobles only (the latter if particularly generous in donations to a given edifice) to be buried within a cult building, a fact which, while suggesting a process of great consequence, also indicates that several attempts must have occurred (and succeeded) to evade the regulations in force.[66]

Archaeology can, undoubtedly, add considerably to the research in this sense, especially when backed by other kinds of written sources (*e.g.* Gregory the Great's *Dialogues*), where, if the presence of graves in sacred places is taken for granted, some measures come out at the same time, in accordance with official ordinances and aiming at limiting and ruling over customs which were taking root across a wider social context. The belief that spiritual salvation was somehow easier if the actual mortal remains lay in religious buildings as well as close to the tombs of saints and martyrs tombs over the suburb, must in the end have affected such a habit in a conclusive way. There are colourful tales about demons exhuming corpses of unworthy clergymen or wicked nobles and throwing them beyond the sacred ground; and not only clergy and nobles, as was the case with a certain dyer, for whom the prohibition was expressly because of his belonging to a lower class.[67] The material records are not in conflict with the literary sources and field-survey often detects a typological discrepancy between burials arranged at a certain distance and those close to or inside churches (the former are usually *cappuccina*, *amphora* or without coffins, and differ sometimes considerably from the latter, and very privileged, tombs, featuring carefully made structures and containing grave goods and garments that, when present, were generally more precious and varied).[68]

The evolution of the funerary practice outlines a fairly variable picture until the beginning of the 8th century, alternating custom and regulations, and achieving a more defined framework only in the Carolingian era proper, when, among the urban contexts, the place of eternal repose is linked firmly to place of prayer.[69] Before that time, on the contrary, there are several examples which clearly appear not only as not following the ecclesiastical instructions, but also did not conform to any organization relevant to public or demesne.

Concerning this, the find of some groups of tombs should be emphasised, whether (eventually) isolated or specifically related to private plots. In interpreting them, one ought not to overlook the possibility that they were associated with nearby houses that have disappeared as a result of the perishable building material used.[70] In certain cases evidence would be direct, as emerges, for instance, from the excavations of the *Palazzo Tabarelli* at *Trent*, or from that of *St. Salvatore* at *Brescia*. The former contains residences with an inner courtyard between, where some graves were located during the 6th and 7th centuries, while at the latter some burials were connected with Longobard dwelling structures, presenting a situation, which, albeit pertinent to state (royal) lands, seems however to be independent from the category mentioned above; fig.23.[71]

The phenomenon shows a complexity and variety of solutions that do not all have complete explanations; some are also obviously lacking in archaeological data and background information. Changes in behaviour, religious ideas and socio-economical factors as a whole therefore contributed to, and brought about, the transformations that occurred throughout the transition centuries. Over this period the sense of town *decorum* also declined substantially, and, as is the cases mentioned previously, a certain pragmatism was, roughly speaking, preferred. It is significant that amongst some peripheral milieux, such as Gaul, marked by a less deeply-rooted urban heritage, these solutions were opted for even during Roman times.[72]

The graves by *St. Giulia*'s at *Brescia*, however, are not to be regarded as a new 'pattern', perhaps brought in by Germanic people, since the Lombards were totally assimilated and intermingled too with that programme that was finally to acknowledge the Church as the leader in the matter of managing town burials (already

---

[65] It is noteworthy that none of them is before the second half of the 6th century, whereas late-Imperial (*Theodosian*-Age) laws warned only against tombs encumbering roads and urban public spaces (Lambert, in Paroli 1997, p.288, note 21 and p.287).

[66] Meneghini – Santangeli Valenzani, 1995, p.285.

[67] *Ib.*, p.285. The bad reputation had by dyers throughout the Middle Ages must have contributed as well (see Pastoureau 2004, pp.156-foll.). In addition to the dyer and the '*malus*' *Valentinus* from Rome, a certain *patricius Valerianus* from *Brescia* can also be mentioned (Wataghin – Lambert, in Brogiolo – Wataghin 1998, p.106 and note 121).

[68] A striking example comes from Rome, where a recently surveyed cemetery shows a marked variance in the form of improved techniques and quality of the burials, which, from the *nymphaeum* nearby *Horti Liciniani*, approached the church of *St. Bibian*. Close to the front, three sarcophagi have been excavated – one of marble and two of terracotta, one of which even contained some golden threads; *ib.*, p.284. Such examples also have parallels elsewhere, *i.e.* at the Longobard *necropolis* of *St. Martino* at *Trezzo sull'Adda*; Lusuardi Siena, in Paroli 1997, p.371.

[69] Wataghin, in Brogiolo 1996, pp.34-35.

[70] Brogiolo – Gelichi 1998, pp.99-100. Such could also be said of those 'petty churches', to which some groups of tombs found at Rome may be linked, according to Fasola's suggestion (1989, pp.1203-foll.); see, however, Pani Ermini's objections (*ib.*, in the round-table discussion).

[71] For *Trent*, Cavada, in Brogiolo – Wataghin 1998, p.133; for *Brescia*, among the others, Brogiolo – Gelichi 1998, pp.99-100. Alternatively, with regard to some burials at *Luni*, Ward Perkins is uncertain whether they were eventually to be attributed to the nearby houses (6th century), taking into account that some graves could be even later than the 10th century (quoted by Brogiolo – Gelichi 1998, p.100).

[72] Lambert, in Paroli 1997, p.287, note 11.

controlled by it in the suburbs) as well as the rituals of inhumation and commemoration of the dead. Diverse socio-political implications must have fostered such an interaction and should be considered in that light (owing to *propaganda* purposes, or in order to consolidate the kingdom and encourage the assimilation of the local Roman culture), so that, if the Bavarian dynasty represented an essential milestone in respect of funeral customs adopted by royal and aristocratic members, a relationship with a cult site, nonetheless, can be noticed not only from early on, as with *Cleph* and *Authari*,[73] but even in later (*Grimuald, Ansprand*) in that troubled period in which struggles over the crown and attempts at establishing new power lineages might well have also yielded other solutions.[74]

*Theodelinda* founded, close to her palace at *Monza*, the religious complex of *St. Giovanni* (where she was eventually interred), and thereby creating a model that could be imitated, the closest parallel being from the Merovingian context and dating from the time of *Radegonde*[75] onwards. Nevertheless, in contrast to the Frankish policy, in Italy such a trend was not promoted (not to say imposed) from above, but, thanks to the conditions offered by the ecclesiastical system, the Longobardic ruling classes realized spontaneously the advantage this kind of investment may have represented for their social and financial interests (in particular, monasteries and religious buildings intended as a means to consolidate properties, in a more profitable and independent way, and for women, above all, to prevent assets and family estates from dispersal.[76]

Furthermore, in an excellent essay on the will of *Rottopert* (745), La Rocca illustrates rightly how the Church also succeeded in gradually superseding the old Germanic burial customs, so that their traditional funeral habits slowly transformed into the Christian ritual proper. One of the most striking examples of the change in progress is, undoubtedly, the abandonment of placing

grave goods with the dead, as the *mobilia* became *post obitum, pro anima* donations, thence part of a bargain and a barter, in order to reach a position in the next world, which well mirrored the idea of power and social relationships amongst the Longobard aristocracy.[77]

By the second half of the 7th century, as the archaeology records, the number of items from tombs sharply decreased until they eventually disappeared, following on from an evolution (stages of which would be shown by the presence of a 'symbolic outfit')[78] that will then have brought individuals to display their social status by means of religious foundations instead of funerary goods, the old Germanic investment *par excellence.*[79]

A final note should be made about the reintroduction of the practice of providing the dead with some objects associated with the indigenous population, as sometimes occurred, a tradition that had disappeared for almost three centuries, possibly a result of the cultural influence of the Lombards, even though, in certain cases, it may be looked upon as a distinguishing feature of the local population in the light of imminent conquest. There are examples of this from *Abruzzi*, where *Crecchio*-type pots have been found in graves; moreover there is some evidence from the excavated site of *Priamàr*, near *Savona*. A few small funerary jugs, made in *Liguria* or North Africa and dating back to the span between the turn of the 6th and the early 7th centuries, would have represented there a sign of either Roman or Byzantine identity, over a region under the threat of Germanic attacks.[80]

Apart from these specific circumstances, however, the study of grave goods might well shed light not only on ritual and social developments, but also on eventual economic exchanges (as indicated by the data from *Crypta Balbi*) in order to acquire in the end important information about the production network, centres and trade routes that seem at times to echo the *scenario* outlined in the 4th century by the establishment of state

---

[73] Lusuardi Siena – Giostra – Spalla, in Brogiolo (ed.) 2000, pp.278 and foll. *Alboin* was buried inside the Palace of *Verona* (where he had wielded power), but such a usage did not survive. *Cleph* and *Authari* were buried in an early Christian church founded by a bishop (*St. Gervasio and Protasio*'s at *Pavia*), as was the Aryan *Rothari* (in the suburban church of *St. Giovanni in Borgo*), while, with *Theodolind*, the custom of burying the founder in his own cult-building was followed, although from the documents it emerges that these edifices were not intended as *mausoleums* at the time they were planned and erected. In the end, it must be remembered that the lack of any archaeological evidence concerning the graves of kings entails the sole use of written sources (except for a few records such as a funerary inscription possibly relevant to *Cunipert*), supported at times by the more abundant finds of tombs of the nobility, which, however, must have accurately followed the royal model (*ib.*, p.274).

[74] The funeral places chosen by *Grimuald* (*St. Ambrogio*'s Church at *Pavia*) and *Ansprand* (*St. Adriano*'s) were different from those of *Aripert I* and his descendants (*St. Salvatore* at *Pavia*). This fact also suggests the sharp break that occurred with the previous royal dynasty, which well mirrored a bloody accession to the throne after civil strife (*ib.*, p.280).

[75] See *infra* text and note 36.

[76] La Rocca, in Paroli 1997, p.13.

[77] *Ib.*, p.23: one's standing was based on the ability to keep and maintain (by means of gifts, pacts, agreements) considerable social and political relationships, so as to be able then to create and strengthen a network of alliances and allegiances. Prestige was not therefore acquired by holding an important office, as happened amongst the Romans, so that taking up an ecclesiastical career marked a big change for Longobard nobles (about Tuscany see Gelichi 1999, p.80).

[78] Concerning this, of note is the find of an arrowhead from one of the high-status graves placed near the *mausoleum* edifice of *St. Martino* at *Trezzo sull'Adda*, which may be considered a symbolic remembrance of ancient funerary weapons (sword, *scramasax, etc.*); Lusuardi Siena, in Paroli 1997, pp.371 and foll.).

[79] See *infra* note 27.

[80] For the Region of *Abruzzi*, Staffa, in Paroli 1997, pp.120-21; about *Priamàr*, Lavagna – Varaldo, in Gelichi (ed.) 1997, p.300 (where other eventual parallels are stressed with *St. Antonino di Perti* as well as other sites of the *Maritima Italorum*).

*fabricae* (*cf.*, for instance, the aforesaid manufacture of bossed shields).[81]

---

[81] See Chapter 1, note 72 and Citter, in Paroli 1997, pp.198-foll. With regards to Tuscany, whilst certain finds interestingly support the idea of interregional trade and manufacture, on the other hand a number of items seem to refer strictly to local workshops (for example, the *Grancia*-type disk-shaped buckle; *ib.*, p.196).

# Conclusions

Archaeology has turned out to be an essential analytical tool for the study of towns, particularly helpful for showing that, as early as Late Antiquity, those conditions arose which also affected the urban (and rural) development of the following period. The centuries of transition (5th-7th), in fact, have recently drawn great attention and interest; the High Middle Ages, on the other hand, still lack, in part, advanced and full research, that might eventually detect how new conjunctures took shape through the slow and complicated process towards the eventual city-state.[1]

This work does not constitute an exception and, as regards the geographical and chronological context, attempts have been made at focussing on the most significant elements, aiming to produce possible lines of investigation about the end of the Antique world and the problems of the ensuing era in evidence at the beginnings of Medieval and Modern Europe.

One of the most individual aspects is undoubtedly the Christianization of society, and field-surveys offer genuine support in understanding how the Church established its material structures among urban frameworks, especially concerning the *ecclesia mater*. New scientific results have allowed scholars to revise previous hypotheses,[2] in particular about its location, and also, in the light of the possible shift (stressed at several times) of some ancient centres towards other nuclear and spun-off districts (*i.e.* attractive ecclesiastical areas) that appear not to have been strictly conditioned afterwards by the Republican or early Imperial planning and defensive walls.[3]

Wherever precise stratigraphical data are available, in fact, the 'cathedral' seems to have usually been erected amidst long-inhabited (and not cemetery) zones,[4] often characterised by a certain 'vitality', as would emerge from those cases that appear close, to and connected with, important roads (Florence), with centres of civil power

(*Brescia*), or with rising economic quarters (*Luni, Ravenna-Classe*).[5]

At the same time, archaeology has yielded a remarkable contribution to the knowledge of some social and cultural aspects relevant to the religious context, by means of a more and more accurate and enlarged study of ritual items. Apart from shedding light on production and trade (both local and interregional),[6] such an approach can well show the stages of any change affecting customs and funeral habits (for instance the disappearance of grave goods), progressively influenced by the Church, whose policy fluctuated between 'adaptation' and 'interference' at least until the 8th century, when more defined rules were finally established over official services,[7] as well as over urban burials (since then strictly related to cult buildings).[8]

The presence of tombs inside the town has often been assumed as a sign of negligence and abandonment of the areas where that phenomenon had taken place, usually explained as coming from wartime emergencies – plausibly one of the main causes in specific circumstances (Rome).[9] Nevertheless, scholars have recently put this interpretation into perspective,[10] even if a large change should be pointedly asserted in respect of urban organization, and, at the same time, of building solutions, as marked by different and poorer typologies (sometimes also connected with graves),[11] for which the reasons can be manifold.

Foreign influences alone can hardly justify the great extent of their spread,[12] moreover the 'new course' seems to have already begun and affected in a conclusive way the ancient *municipia*, as well as the territorial patterns, some time before the invasion of the Longobards

---

[1] Wickham, in Francovich – Noyé 1994, p.757.
[2] Based nearly exclusively on literary sources (sometimes not correctly interpreted): *cf.* Testini 1989, pp.9-foll.
[3] For the problem of city walls during Late Antiquity, see Chapter 2, in particular notes 18, 26 and 39-42.
[4] In Florence, at the cult site of *St. Reparata*, the only exactly dated graves (Longobard era) are contemporaneous with, or later, than the church, since they impinge upon the latter. Such a point does not allow for the relocation of the 'cathedral' to (formerly) a cemetery area, but the religious building itself must have attracted a number of burials (Testini 1989, p.63). Likewise it is worth considering the Longobard tombs exposed after digging at *Piazza del Duomo* at *Pisa*, possibly relating to the pre-*Buscheto* edifice (Alberti – Baldassarri, 1999, pp.369 and foll., who take into account also the survey results obtained by Pani Ermini in 1985).

[5] Chapter 3, note 15, for other examples too.
[6] Chapter 3, note 81.
[7] It is noticeable that Late Antique grave goods cannot be related to a wholly Christian identity. This could reveal the existing, and significant, importance of local and family traditions in such ceremonies; nevertheless there was slight interest of the Church in regulating this matter during that time (Gastaldo, in Brogiolo – Wataghin 1998, p.32). Conversely, in the 7th to the 8th centuries, clergymen will have acted together with (and finally for) private individuals (usually women) while officiating at funeral rites (evidence in this sense emerges from ceremonies concerning Longobard nobles): La Rocca, in Paroli 1997, p.22.
[8] Brogiolo – Gelichi 1998, p.101.
[9] Large burial grounds like that of *St. Eusebius* on the *Esquiline* Hill sprang up no sooner than the Greek-Gothic War (see Chapter 3, note 54).
[10] Brogiolo – Gelichi 1998, p.100.
[11] *Ib.*, pp.99-100.
[12] Let's remember, for instance, the *Grubenhäuser* of Byzantine *Apulia* (Chapter 2, note 72).

themselves, so that also other factors may be looked for – mainly social and economic. The utilization of certain materials and the return of prehistoric dwellings should then be considered in the light of a general increase in poverty. In addition the technical background of 'rustic' tradition sometimes found, would possibly indicate the coming of rural people to city; this is likely to be a result of war, insecurity, and thus leading to the ensuing weakness of country production systems.[13]

Concerning this, the widespread use of timber is obviously one of the most striking indicators, which would have reached a very high construction standard throughout the mid- and late-Early Middle-Ages (*i.e.* the strong, elegant examples from *Ferrara* and, above all, *Bologna*).[14] However, as regards the transition centuries, it would rather denote a certain 'regression' (as also the use of other perishable materials, such as turf, might indicate). This might be supported in the end by the association of timber with a coarsening of urban structures and services[15] and, in some extreme cases (inland *Abruzzi*), even with the emergence of rural forms of organization within the boundaries of what had been the territory and scope of the ancient town.[16]

Amongst the eventual and direct causes of changes that took place during Late Antiquity, stands out the different (diminished) resource allocation, the result of new defensive measures and diverse territorial operations (from strategic and political necessities), particularly urgent by the time of the Tetrarchic era.[17] *Castra* or fortified sites may therefore have drawn greater 'attention', partly at the expense of some towns, where, what is more, long-term crises could no longer be checked by a strong (Roman) government.

In this sense, certain data relevant to pottery finds should also be considered (*St. Antonino di Perti*), as well as those breaks in the middle of the 5th, 6th and 7th centuries (Wickham) that show quite a sharp drop in trading levels, and which would at first have hit the 'weakest', peripheral areas and become progressively widespread over most of the regions.[18]
Furthermore, merchandise seems to have travelled through the routes specifically maintained for military purposes, as Constantinople probably tried to keep all the districts under the imperial influence connected with each other within an active commercial network (Christie).[19] On this matter, an interesting question arises, whether (and to what extent) African and Oriental commodities really mirrored local economic strength, or, in most cases, should be seen exclusively in the light of strategic requirements, considering that, once out of the Byzantine sphere (*Maritima Italorum*), such regions were generally affected by a steep fall in imports.[20]

Another issue concerns the significance of pottery, in particular whether this may be asserted (even during the Transition period) as an 'independent economic variable', as has been properly put forward by Wickham for the following Early Medieval centuries (a period in which the prosperity of some geographical contexts does not seem to be fully corroborated by ceramics). No fine/high-quality products come from northern Italy (in some sites until the Late Middle Ages) – nothing at least that can ever be comparable with the so-called *Forum* Ware, which was widespread during the 8th century over the central and southern areas of the peninsula. By contrast, architectural and literary evidence indicate situations that appear to have been anything but recessive.[21]

Commerce (and, indirectly, the relevant craft workshops) is proved to a considerable extent (*i.e.* relationships between southern France and some Italian districts),[22] but it can hardly be assumed, however, as an immediate cause of that 'outburst of prosperity', observed by Barnish about the 8th-/9th-century *Po*-Valley regions.[23] Scholars rather stress the soundness of agricultural systems that were based on territorial reorganization, and carried out by towns, *curtes* and ecclesiastical institutions (*i.e.*, monasteries), on those lands that had long been locked in within the properties of Longobard kings and dukes.[24]

A consistent and steady production surplus would have allowed, on the other hand, even different kinds of investment opportunities. Therefore further studies may help to establish whether eventual riches hoarded by merchant activity (as was the case with the Doge of Venice *Partecipatio*, attested by written sources)[25] can ever be seen at the heart of later processes, throwing some light so on the final centuries of the Early Middle Ages, an epoch marked by several changes and breaks that seem to have been absolutely 'in transition'.[26]

---

[13] *Cf.* Chapter 2, note 76.
[14] *Cf.* Chapter 2, note 102.
[15] Restoration (which however brings witness of previous disuse) as well as a certain care of water and sewerage systems, usually (if not exclusively) indicated cities of some importance: for example the capitals (Milan, *Ravenna, Pavia*); see Chapter 2, notes 82, 83.
[16] Chapter 2, note 66.
[17] *Cf.* Chapter 2, note 61. Of interest is Whittaker's idea suggesting that trade was directly managed by the civil authority and the great landowners throughout Late Antiquity, based on an economy under state control; this might also reflect a society that was definitely more militarised (see Chapter 1, Final Remarks and note 71).
[18] Wickham, 1999, p.1 and foll.: Among the main causes for the decrease in commerce, must be stressed the end of tributes previously paid by the provinces and the 'maritime traffic organised by the Roman state in order to supply Italy and Rome itself with African corn' (Delogu, in Francovich – Noyé 1994, p.9).

[19] See Chapter 1, note 45.
[20] Gardini – Murialdo, in Francovich – Noyé 1994, p.170.
[21] Brogiolo – Gelichi 1998, p.41.
[22] *Cf.* Chapter 1, note 48. It should be noted that the large spread of *Salerno* thick-glaze-coated pottery would indicate the growth of that town and its port (at the expense of Naples) since the 8th century (see Chapter 1, note 29).
[23] Chapter 1, note 29 and Brogiolo – Gelichi 1998, p.43.
[24] This topic is well summarised by Brogiolo – Gelichi 1998, p.42 and 159-60.
[25] *Ib.*, p.42.
[26] *Introduction*, in Christie – Loseby 1996, p.1.

# References

**Abbreviations:**

"**AM**": "Archeologia Medievale", I, (1974-).
"**NSAL**": "Notiziario della Soprintendenza Archeologica della Lombardia", 1981- 1994.
**Settimane di Studio...Spoleto**: Settimane di Studio del Centro Italiano di Studio sull'Alto Medioevo, Spoleto (1954-).

Alberti A., Baldassarri M., *Per la storia dell'insediamento longobardo a Pisa: nuovi materiali dall'area cimiteriale di piazza del Duomo*, "AM", XXVI, 1999, pp.369-76.

Alberti A., *Produzione e commercializzazione della pietra ollare in Italia settentrionale tra tardo antico e alto medioevo*, in Gelichi (ed.) 1997, pp.335-39.

Andrews D., Pringle D., *Lo scavo dell'area sud del Convento di S. Silvestro a Genova*, "AM", IV, 1977, pp.47-207.

Andrews D., Pringle D., Cartledge I., *Lo scavo dell'area sud del chiostro di S. Silvestro a Genova*, "AM", V, 1978, pp.415-51.

Arthur P., Whitehouse D., *Appunti sulla produzione laterizia nell'Italia centromeridionale tra il IV e il XII secolo*, "AM", X, 1983, pp.525-37.

Arthur P., *Naples: a case of urban survival in early medieval ages?*, "Mèlanges de l'Ecole Francaise de Rome. Moyen Age", 103, 1991, pp.709-784.

Arthur P. (ed.), *Il complesso archeologico di Carminiello ai Mannesi. Napoli (scavi 1983-1984)*, 1994, Lecce.

Arthur P., Patterson H., *Ceramics and early Medieval central and Southern Italy: "a potted history"*, in Francovich – Noyé (eds.) 1994, pp.409-441.

Arthur P., *Grubenhauser nella Puglia bizantina. A proposito di recenti scavi a Supersano (LE)*, "AM", XXVI, 1999, pp.171-78.

Arthur P., *Naples, from Roman town to city-state: an archaeological perspective*, London, published by The British school at Rome, in association with the Dipartimento di Beni Culturali, Università degli studi di Lecce, 2002.

Augenti A., *Il Palatino nell'alto Medioevo*, in Francovich – Noyè (eds.), 1994, pp.659-91.

Augenti A. (ed.), *Le città italiane tra la tarda Antichità e l'alto Medioevo*, Atti del convegno (Ravenna, 26-28 February 2004), 2004.

Baggio Bernardoni M., *Trento: Porta Veronensis*, "Quaderni di Archeologia del Veneto", XIII, 1997, pp.239-40.

Balzaretti R., *Cities, emporia: local economics in the Po valley, c. 700-875*, in Christie – Loseby (eds.), 1996, pp.212-234.

Bandmann G., *Early Medieval Architecture as bearers of meaning*, Columbia University Press, New York (USA), 2005.

Barnish S.J.B., *The transformation of classical cities and the Pirenne debate*, "Journal of Roman Archaeology", 1989, pp.385-400.

Barnish S.J.B., *Conclusioni*, in Brogiolo (ed.) 1996, pp.181-87.

Bastianoni C., Cherubini G., Pinto G. (eds.). Final edition by C. Nenci, *La Toscana ai tempi di Arnolfo*, Atti del convegno di Studi Colle di Val d'Elsa, 22-24 November 2002, Leo S. Olschki Editore, 2005.

Belli Barsali I., *La topografia di Lucca nei secoli VIII-IX*, Atti del V Convegno Internazionale di Studi sull'Alto Medioevo (Lucca 1971), Spoleto, 1974, pp.461-552.

Bergonzini G.D. *et al.*, *La successione stratigrafica rilevata nei recenti sondaggi presso l'abside centrale del Duomo*, in *Modena dalle origini all'anno Mille. Studi di archeologia e storia*, Modena, pp.463-65.

Bernacchia R., *I Longobardi nelle Marche. Problemi di storia dell'insediamento e delle istituzioni (secoli VIVIII)*, in Paroli (ed.) 1997, pp.9-30.

Biagini M., Melli P., Torre E., *La ceramica comune in Liguria nel VI-VII secolo: Genova*, in Saguì (ed.) 1998, pp.577-84.

Bianchi L., *Roma: strutture fortificate medioevali in rapporto all'antica viabilità di accesso all'Esquilino e loro sopravvivenza...*, in Gelichi (ed.) 1997, pp.86-91.

Bierbrauer V., *Die Kontinuitaet staedtischen Lebens in Oberitalien aus archaeologischer Sicht (5.-7./8. Jahrhundert)*, in *Die Stadt in Oberitalien und in den norwestlischen Provinzen des Roemischen Reiches*, Mainz am Rheim, 1991, pp.263-86.

Binding G., *Medieval Building Techniques*, Tempus, Stroud (UK), 2000.

Blake H., Maccabruni C., *Lo scavo a Villa Maria di Lomello (Pavia)*, "AM", XII, 1985, pp.189-212.

Bognetti G.P., *Problemi di metodo e oggetti di studio nella storia delle città italiane dell'alto medioevo*, VI Settimana di Studi sull'alto medioevo (Spoleto 1958), Spoleto, 1959, pp. 59-87.

Bognetti G.P., *S. Maria foris portas di Castelseprio e la Storia religiosa dei Longobardi*, in *L'età dei Longobardi*, II, 1966.

Boldrini E., Parenti R. (eds.), *Santa Maria della Scala. Archeologia e edilizia sulla piazza dello Spedale*, 1992, Firenze.

Brambilla M., Brogiolo G.P., *Case altomedievali dell'isola Comacina*, "AM", XXI, 1994, pp.463-67.

Bratoz R., *Il cristianesimo aquileiese prima di Costantino*, 1999, Udine.

Braudel F., *Civiltà e imperi del Mediterraneo nell'età di Filippo II*, updated edition, 1982, vol. I.

Brogiolo G.P. (ed.), *Archeologia urbana in Lombardia*, Modena, 1984.

Brogiolo G.P., *La città tra tarda antichità e altomedioevo*, in Brogiolo (ed.) 1984, pp.48-56.

Brogiolo G.P., *Brescia. La città tra tarda antichità e altomedioevo: la crescita della stratificazione*, in Brogiolo (ed.) 1984, pp.88-91.

Brogiolo G.P., *A proposito dell'organizzazione urbana nell'altomedioevo*, "AM", XIV, 1987, pp.27-46.

Brogiolo G.P., *Brescia: building transformations in a Lombard city*, in Randsborg (ed.), 1989, pp.156-65.

Brogiolo G.P., *Brescia altomedievale. Urbanistica ed edilizia dal IV al IX secolo*, 1993, Mantova.

Brogiolo G.P. (ed.), *Edilizia abitativa altomedievale in Italia centrosettentrionale*, Atti del IV seminario sul tardoantico e l'altomedioevo in Italia centrosettentrionale (Monte Barro 1993), 1994, Mantova.

Brogiolo G.P., *Edilizia residenziale in Lombardia (V-VIII secolo)*, in Brogiolo (ed.) 1994, pp.103-14.

Brogiolo G.P. (ed.), *Città, castelli e campagne nei territori di confine (secc. VI-VII)*, Atti del V seminario sul tardoantico e l'altomedioevo in Italia centrosettentrionale (Monte Barro 1994), 1995, Mantova.

Brogiolo G.P. (ed.), *Early medieval towns in the Western Mediterranean*, (Atti del Convegno, Ravello 1994), 1996, Mantova.

Brogiolo G.P., *Considerazioni sulle sequenze altomedievali nella zona monumentale della città romana*, in Rossi (ed.) 1996, pp.257-63.

Brogiolo G.P., *Prospettive per l'archeologia dell'architettura*, "Archeologia dell'architettura", I, 1996, pp.11-15.

Brogiolo G.P., *Le sepolture a Brescia tra tarda antichità e prima età longobarda (ex IV-VII)*, in Paroli (ed.) 1997, pp.413-24.

Brogiolo G.P. (ed.), *Le fortificazioni del Garda e i sistemi di difesa dell'Italia settentrionale tra Tardo antico e Alto medioevo*, 1999.

Brogiolo G.P., *Un'enclave bizantine sul lago di Garda?*, in Brogiolo (ed.) 1999, pp.13-20.

Brogiolo G.P. (ed.), Atti del II Congresso Nazionale di Archeologia Medievale, Firenze, 2000.

Brogiolo G.P., *Urbanistica di Cividale longobarda, Paolo Diacono e il Friuli Altomedievale (secc.VI-X)*, Atti del XIV Congresso internazionale di studi sull'Alto Medioevo, Cividale del Friuli-Bottenicco di Mainacco 24-29 September 1999, Spoleto, 2001, pp.357-85.

Brogiolo G.P., Cremaschi M., Gelichi S., *Processi di stratificazione in centri urbani (dalla stratificazione "naturale" alla stratificazione "archeologica")*, "Archeologia stratigrafica dell'Italia settentrionale", I, 1996, pp.23-30.

Brogiolo G.P., Cuni C., *Le sepolture di età longobarda di S. Giulia in Brescia*, "Rivista di studi liguri", anno LIV-N.1-4, January-December 1988, pp.145-58.

Brogiolo G.P., Delogu P. (eds.), *L'Adriatico dalla tarda antichità all'età carolingia*, Atti del convegno di studio (Brescia 11-13 October 2001), Firenze, 2005.

Brogiolo G.P., Gauthier N., Christie N. (eds.), *Towns and their territories between Late Antiquity and the Early Middle Ages*, Brill Academic Publishers, Amsterdam, 2000.

Brogiolo G.P., Gelichi S. (eds.), *Le ceramiche alto medievali (fine VI-X secolo) in Italia settentrionale: produzione e commerci*, 1996.

Brogiolo G.P., Gelichi S., *La Ceramica comune in Italia settentrionale tra IV e VII secolo*, in Saguì (ed.) 1998, pp.209-26.

Brogiolo G.P., Gelichi S., *La città nell'alto medioevo italiano. Archeologia e storia*, 1998.

Brogiolo G.P., Ward Perkins B., *The Idea and Ideal of the Town between Late Antiquity and the Early Middle Ages*, Brill Academic Publishers, Amsterdam, 1999.

Brogiolo G.P., Cantino Wataghin G. (eds.), *Sepolture tra IV e VIII secolo*, 1998.

Buora M., *Osservazioni sulle sepolture ad Aquileia*, in Cuscito – Verzàr Bass (eds.) 2004, pp.379-400.

Cagiano de Azevedo M., *Aspetti urbanistici delle città altomedievali*, XXI Settimana di Studi sull'alto medioevo (Spoleto 1973), Spoleto, 1974, pp.641-77.

Cagnana A., *Archeologia della produzione fra tardo-antico e altomedioevo: le tecniche murarie e l'organizzazione dei cantieri*, in Brogiolo (ed.) 1994, pp.39-52.

Cagnana, *La transizione al medioevo attraverso la storia delle tecniche murarie: dall'analisi di un territorio a un problema sovraregionale*, in Gelichi (ed.) 1997, pp.445-48.

Cagnana A., Roascio S., *Indagini archeologiche nella chiesa di San Paolo di Illegio (UD): le fasi tardo-antiche e altomedievali*, in Francovich (ed.), Atti del IV Congresso Nazionale di Archeologia Medievale, San Galgano-Siena, September 2006, pp.304-10.

Cantini F., *Archeologia urbana a Siena. L'area dell'Ospedale di Santa Maria prima dell'ospedale. Altomedioevo*, Firenze, 2005.

Cantino Wataghin G., *"Urbs" e "civitas" nella tarda antichità: linee di ricerca*, in La "Civitas Christiana". Urbanistica delle città italiane fra tarda antichità e altomedioevo, I Seminario di studio (Turin 1991), 1992, pp.7-42.

Cantino Wataghin G., *L'edilizia abitativa tardoantica e altomedievale nell'Italia nord-occidentale. "Status quaestionis"*, in Brogiolo (ed.) 1994, pp.89-102.

Cantino Wataghin G., *Spazio cristiano e "civitates": "status quaestionis"*, in Materiali per una topografia urbana. "Status quaestionis" e nuove acquisizioni, V Convegno sull'archeologia tardoromana e medievale in Sardegna (Cagliari-Cuglieri 1988), Oristano, 1995, pp.201-39.

Cantino Wataghin G., *Archeologia dei monasteri. L'Altomedioevo*, in Gelichi (ed.) 1997, pp.265-68.

Cantino Wataghin G., Gurt Espaguerra J.M., Guyon J., *Topografia della "civitas christiana" tra IV e VI secolo*, in Brogiolo (ed.) 1996, pp.17-43.

Cantino Wataghin G., Lambert C., *Sepolture e città. L'Italia settentrionale tra IV e VIII secolo*, in Brogiolo – Wataghin (eds.) 1998, pp.89-114.

Cantino Wataghin G., *...ut haec aedes Cristo Domino in Ecclesiam consecretur. Il riuso cristiano di edifici antichi tra tarda antichità e alto medioevo*, Settimane di Studio...Spoleto 1999, pp.673-750.

Cantino Wataghin G., *La città tardoantica: il caso di Aquileia*, in Cuscito – Verzàr Bass (eds.) 2004, pp.101-19.

Caporosso D. (ed.), *Scavi MM3. Ricerche di archeologia urbana a Milano durante la costruzione della linea 3 della Metropolitana 1982-1990*, 1991.

Cappelli F., *Le origini della cattedrale di Ascoli*, in Paroli (ed.) 1997, pp.81-90.

Carter M., *Archeologia urbana in Europa*, in Brogiolo (ed.) 1984, pp.9-21.

Carver M, *Arguments in stone. Archaeological research and the european towns in the first millennium*, 1993, Oxford.

Castagna D., Tirelli M., *Evidenze archeologiche di Oderzo tardoantica ed altomedievale: i risultati preliminari di recenti indagini*, in Brogiolo (ed.) 1995, pp.121-34.

Catarsi Dall'Aglio M., *Evidenze archeologiche altomedievali a Parma e nel suo territorio*, in *Testimonianze archeologiche altomedievali nella provincia di Parma*, 1992, Parma, pp.1-13.

Catarsi Dall'Aglio M., *Edilizia fra tardoantico e alto medioevo. L'esempio dell'Emilia occidentale*, in Brogiolo (ed.) 1994, pp.149-56.

Catarsi Dall'Aglio M., Dall'Aglio P.L., *Le città dell'Emilia Occidentale tra Tardoantico e Altomedioevo*, "Studi e Documenti di Archeologia", VII, 1991-92, pp.9-29.

Cavada E., *Cimiteri e sepolture isolate nella città di Trento (secoli V-VIII)*, in Brogiolo – Wataghin (eds.) 1998, pp.123-42.

Cavalieri Manasse G., Hudson P.J., *Nuovi dati sulle fortificazioni di Verona (III-IX secolo)*, in Brogiolo (ed.) 1999, pp.71-92.

Celuzza M.G., Fentress E., *La Toscana centro-meridionale: i casi di Cosa-Ansedonia e Roselle*, in Francovich – Noyè (eds.) 1994, pp.601-13.

Chevalier P., *Salona II. Ecclesiae Dalmatiae. La architecture paleochrètienne de la Province romaine de Dalmatie (IV-VII s.)*, 2, 1995, Roma-Split.

Christie N., *The Limes bizantino reviewed: the defence of Liguria, AD 568-643*, "Rivista di studi liguri", anno LV-N.1-4, January-December 1989, pp.5-38.

Christie N., *The city walls of Ravenna: the defence of a Capital, AD 402-750*, "XXXVI Corso di Cultura sull'Arte Ravennate e Bizantina", 1989, Ravenna, pp.113-38.

Christie N., *Byzantine Liguria: an imperial province against the Longobards, AD 568-643*, "Papers British School at Rome", LVIII, 1990, pp.229-71.

Christie N., Loseby S.T. (eds.), *Towns in transition. Urban evolution in Late Antiquity and the Early Middle Ages*, 1996, Sabon.

Christie N., Rustworth A., *Urban fortification and defensive strategy in fifth and sixth century Italy: the case of Terracina*, "Journal of Roman Archaeology", I, 1988, pp.73-88.

Ciampoltrini G., Notini P., *Lucca tardoantica e altomedievale: nuovi contributi archeologici*, "AM", XVII, 1990, pp.561-90.

Ciampoltrini G., *Città "frammentate" e città-fortezza. Storie urbane della Toscana centro-settentrionale fra Teodosio e Carlo Magno*, in Francovich Noyè (eds.) 1994, pp.615-33.

Ciampoltrini G., *Tecniche di reimpiego e modelli architettonici fra tarda antichità e alto medioevo. Divagazioni sulle cattedrali di Chiusi e Roselle*, "AM", XXIX, 2002, pp.441-52.

Cipriano S., Sandrini G.M., *Fornaci e produzioni fittili ad Altino*, in Brogiolo – Olcese (eds.), *Produzione ceramica in area padana tra il II secolo a. C. e il VII d.C.: nuove prospettive di ricerca*, Convegno internazionale di Desenzano del Garda, 8-10 aprile 1999, 2000, pp.189-96.

Citter C., *Rete portuale e commerci nella Toscana costiera tardoantica e altomedievale*, in Brogiolo (ed.) 1996, pp.133-42.

Citter C., *I corredi funebri nella Toscana longobarda...*, in Paroli (ed.) 1997, pp.185-212.

Citter C., *La trasformazione di aree ed edifici pubblici nelle città toscane fra tardo antico e alto medioevo*, in Gelichi (ed.) 1997, pp.27-30.

Citter C., *I corredi nella Tuscia longobarda: produzione locale, dono o commercio?*, in Brogiolo – Cantino Wataghin (eds.) 1998, pp.179-96.

Coates Stephens R., *Quattro torri altomedievali delle mura Aureliane*, "AM", XXII, 1995, pp.501-19.

Coccia S., *Il "Portus Romae" fra tarda antichità e altomedioevo*, in Paroli – Delogu (eds.) 1993, pp.177-202.

Colecchia A., *L'Alto Garda occidentale dalla preistoria al post medioevo. Archeologia, storia del popolamento e trasformazione del paesaggio*, SAP, Mantova, 2005.

Corradini R., Diesenberger M., Reimitz H., *The Construction of the Communities in the Early Middle Ages*, Brill Academic Publishers, Amsterdam, 2004.

Croce Da Villa P. *et alii*, *Concordia Sagittaria: scavo nell'area nord del piazzale*, "Quaderni di Archeologia del Veneto", III, 1987, pp.86-98.

Croce Da Villa P. (ed.), *Il quadriportico della basilica paleocristiana di Concordia Sagittaria*, "Quaderni di Archeologia del Veneto", XVIII, 2002, pp.100-15.

Curina R. *et al.*, *Contesti tardo-antichi e altomedievali dal sito di Villa Clelia (Imola, Bologna)*, "AM", XVII, 1990, pp.121-234.

Cuscito G., Verzàr Bass M. (eds.), *Aquileia dalle origini alla costituzione del ducato longobardo. Topografia – Urbanistica – Edilizia pubblica*, "Antichità Altoadriatiche", LIX, Trieste, 2004.

Cuscito G., *Lo spazio cristiano nell'urbanistica tardoantica di Aquileia*, in Cuscito – Verzàn Bass 2004, pp.511-59.

Cuteri F.A., *La Calabria nell'Alto Medioevo (VI-X secolo)*, in Francovich – Noyé (eds.) 1994, pp.339-60.

Dal Ri L., Rizzi G., *L'edilizia residenziale in Alto Adige tra V e VIII secolo*, in Brogiolo (eds.) 1994, pp.135-48.

Dal Ri L., Rizzi G., *Il territorio altoatesino alla fine del VI e nel VII secolo d.C.*, in Brogiolo (ed.) 1995, pp.87-114.

Degasperi A., *Sepolture urbane e viabilità a Lucca fra tarda antichità e altomedioevo*, "AM", XXII, 1995, pp.537-50.

De Iong M., Thews F., Van Rhijn C., *Topographies of Power in the Early Middle Ages*, Brill Academic Publishers, Amsterdam, 2001.

Delogu P., *Mito di una città meridionale (Salerno, secoli VIII-IX)*, 1977.

Delogu P., *The rebirth of Rome in the eighth and ninth centuries*, in Hodges – Hobley (eds.), *The rebirth of towns in the West. AD 700-1050*, London, 1988, pp.32-42.

Delogu P., *La fine del mondo antico e l'inizio del medioevo: nuovi dati per un vecchio problema*, in Francovich – Noyé (eds.) 1994, pp.7-30.

De Marchi P.M., *Modelli insediativi "militarizzati" d'età longobarda in Lombardia*, in Brogiolo (ed.) 1995, pp.33-86.

De Marchi P.M., *Note su produzioni e scambi nella Lombardia di età longobarda: l'esempio degli scudi da parata*, in Brogiolo (ed.) 2000, pp.284-91.

De Marinis G., Pallecchi P., *Resti di lavorazione vetraria tardo-romana negli scavi di Piazza della Signoria a Firenze*, in Mendera (ed.), *Archeologia e storia della produzione del vetro preindustriale*, Firenze, 1991, pp.55-66.

Demeglio P., *Città e cinte difensive nell'Italia Annonaria*, in *La "Civitas Christiana". Urbanistica delle città italiane fra tarda antichità e altomedioevo*, I Seminario di studio (Turin 1991), 1992, pp.43-53.

Donati P., *Legno, pietra e terra. L'arte del costruire*, 1992, Firenze.

Duprè Thesaider E., *Problemi della città nell'alto medioevo*, VI Settimana di Studi sull'alto medioevo (Spoleto 1958), 1959, pp.15-46.

Esch A., *Le vie di comunicazione di Roma nell'alto medioevo*, Settimane di Studio…Spoleto 2001, pp.421-53.

Fasola U.M., Fiocchi Nicolai V., *Le necropoli durante la formazione della città cristiana*, Actes du XI Congrès International d'Archèologie Chrètienne (Lyon 1986), Rome, 1989, pp.1152-205.

Filippi F., Pejrani L., Subrizio M., *Torino, via Basilica angolo via Conte Verde. Indagine archeologica*, "Quaderni della Soprintendenza Archeologica del Piemonte", 11, 1993, pp.291-93.

Fiocchi Nicolai V., *Elementi di trasformazione dello spazio funerario tra tarda antichità ed altomedioevo*, Settimane di Studio…Spoleto 2003, pp.921-70.

Fontana S., *Le "imitazioni" della sigillata africana e le ceramiche da mensa italiche tardo-antiche*, in Saguì (ed.) 1998, pp.83-100.

Fortunati Zuccala M., *Bergamo. Piazza Rosate e piazzetta Terzi. Aree pluristratificate*, "NSAL", 1990, pp.142-43.

Francovich R., Noyè G. (eds.), *La storia dell'alto medioevo italiano alla luce dell'archeologia*, Convegno Internazionale (Siena 1992), Firenze, 1994.

Fraschetti A., *Il Campidoglio: dal tardoantico all'alto medioevo*, Settimane di Studio…Spoleto 2001, pp.31-56.

Gadd D., Ward Perkins B., *The development of urban domestic housing in north Italy. The evidence of the excavations on the San Romano Site*, Ferrara (1981-84), "The Journal of the Accordia Research Centre", 2, 1991, pp.105-27.

Galetti P., *Una campagna e la sua città. Piacenza e territorio nei secoli VIII-X*, 1994, Bologna.

Galetti P., *Le strutture insediative nelle legislazioni barbariche*, in Brogiolo (ed.) 1994, pp.15-23.

Gandolfi D., *Ceramiche fini di importazione di VI-VII secolo in Liguria. L'esempio di Ventimiglia, Alberga e Luni*, in Saguì (ed.) 1998, pp.253-74.

Gardini A., Melli P., *Necropoli e sepolture urbane ed extraurbane a Genova tra tardo antico ed alto medioevo*, "Rivista di studi liguri", anno LIV, N.1-4, January-December 1988, pp.159-78.

Gardini A., Milanese M., *L'archeologia urbana a Genova negli anni 1964-1978*, "AM", VI, 1979, pp.129-70.

Gardini A., Murialdo G., *La Liguria*, in Francovich – Noyé (eds.) 1994, pp.159-82.

Garzella G., *Pisa com'era: topografia e insediamento dall'impianto tardo antico alla città muraria del secolo XII*, 1990, Napoli.

Gasparri S., *Longobardi e città*, "Società e Storia", 46, 1989, pp.973-79.

Gasparri S., *La frontiera in Italia (secc. VI-VIII)…*, in Brogiolo (ed.) 1995, pp.9-20.

Gasparri S. (ed.), *Il regno dei Longobardi in Italia: archeologia, società e istituzioni*, Fondazione Centro Italiano di Studi sull'Alto Medioevo, Spoleto, 2004.

Gastaldo G., *I corredi funerari nelle tombe "tardo romane" in Italia settentrionale*, in Brogiolo – Cantino Wataghin (eds.) 1998, pp.15-60.

Gelichi S., *Il paesaggio urbano tra V e X secolo*, in A. Carile (ed.), *Storia di Ravenna*, vol. II, *Dall'età bizantina all'età ottoniana*, Venezia, 1991, pp.153-65.

Gelichi S., *La città in EmiliaRomagna tra tardo-antico ed altomedioevo*, in Francovich – Noyè (eds.) 1994, pp.567-600.

Gelichi S., *L'edilizia residenziale in Romagna tra V e VIII secolo*, in Brogiolo (ed.) 1994, pp. 157-67.

Gelichi S., *Territori di confine in età longobarda: l'"ager mutinensis"*, in Brogiolo (ed.), 1995, pp.145-58.

Gelichi S., *Note sulle città bizantine dell'Esarcato e della Pentapoli tra IV e IX secolo*, in Brogiolo (ed.) 1996, pp.67-76.

Gelichi S., *Ceramiche tipo "Classe"*, in Saguì (ed.) 1998, pp.481-86.

Gelichi S., *Le mura inesistenti e la città dimezzata. Note di topografia pisana altomedievale*, "AM", XXV, 1998, pp.75-88.

Gelichi S. *et al.*, *Studi e ricerche archeologiche sul sito altomedievale di Cittanova*, in *Modena dalle origini all'anno Mille. Studi di storia e di archeologia*, vol. I, 1989, Modena, pp.577-603.

Gelichi S., Ortalli G., in *Lo scavo nell'area cortilizia delle Scuole Medie Guinizelli in via S. Isaia*, in Gelichi – Merlo R. (eds.), *Archeologia medievale a Bologna. Gli scavi nel Convento di San Domenico*, 1987, Bologna, pp.50-57.

Gelichi S. (ed.), Atti del I Congresso Nazionale di Archeologia Medievale, Firenze, 1997.

Gelichi S. (ed.), *Archeologia medievale in Emilia occidentale. Ricerche e studi*, 1998.

Gelichi S. (ed.), *Archeologia urbana in Toscana. La città altomedievale*, 1999.

Giuntella A.M., *Note su alcuni aspetti della ritualità funeraria nell'alto medioevo. Consuetudini e innovazioni*, in Brogiolo – Cantino Wataghin (eds.) 1998, pp.61-76.

Gizzi E., Pannuzzi S., *Atri, centro storico: riutilizzo medievale di un isolato romano*, "AM", XV, 1988, pp.587-608.

Godoy Fernandez C., *Baptisterios hispanicos (siglos IV al VIII). Arqueologia y liturgia*, Actes du XI Congrès International d'Archèologie Chrètienne, vol. 1, 1989, Città del Vaticano, pp.607-34.

Guglielmetti A., *La ceramica comune fra fine VI e X secolo a Brescia, nei siti di casa Pallaveri, palazzo Martinengo Cesaresco e piazza Labus*, in Brogiolo – Gelichi (eds.) 1996, pp.9-14.

Hansen I.L., Wickham C., *The long eight century. Production, distribution, demand*, Brill Academic Publishers, Amsterdam, 2000.

Hendy M.F., *East and West: the transformation of Late Roman Financial Structures*, Settimane di Studio…Spoleto 2002, pp.1307-369.

Hobart M., *Cosa-Ansedonia (Orbetello) in età medievale. Rapporto preliminare: da una città romana ad un insediamento medievale sparso*, "AM", XXII, 1995, pp.569-84.

Hodges R., *The rebirth of towns in the early Middle Ages*, in Hodges – Hobley 1988, pp.1-7.

Hodges R.Hobley B., *The rebirth of towns in the West. AD 700-1050*, 1988, London.

Hodges R., *In the Shadow of Pirenne: San Vincenzo al Volturno and the revival of Mediterranean commerce*, in Francovich – Noyé (eds.) 1994, pp.109-28.

Hodges R., *Dream Cities: Emporia and the End of the Dark Ages*, in Christie – Loseby (eds.) 1996.

Hodges R., Bowden W., *The sixth century*, Brill Academic Publishers, Amsterdam, 1998.

Hodges R., *Towns and Trade in the Age of Charlemagne*, Duckworth, London (UK), 2000.

Hudson P.J., *Archeologia urbana e programmazione della ricerca: l'esempio di Pavia*, 1981, Firenze.

Hudson P., *Pavia*, in Brogiolo (ed.) 1984, pp.140-50.

Hudson P.J., *La dinamica dell'insediamento urbano nell'area del cortile del Tribunale di Verona. L'età medievale*, "AM", XII, 1985, pp.281-302.

Hudson P.J., *Pavia: l'evoluzione urbanistica di una capitale altomedievale*, in *Storia di Pavia*, vol. II, Pavia, 1987, pp.237-315.

Hudson P.J., *Contributi archeologici alla storia dell'insediamento urbano veneto*, in Castagnetti A., Varanini G.M. (eds.), *Il Veneto nel Medioevo. Dalla Venetia alla marca veronese*, I, 1989, Verona, pp.329-348.

Hudson P.J., *Le mura romane di Pavia*, in *Mura delle città romane in Lombardia*, Atti del Convegno di Como (1991), 1993, pp.107-18.

Kurze W., Citter C., *La Toscana*, in Brogiolo (ed.) 1995, pp.159-86.

Lambert C., *Sepolture e spazio urbano: proposte per un repertorio*, in *La "Civitas Christiana". Urbanistica delle città italiane fra tarda antichità e alto medioevo*, Torino, 1992, pp.145-58.

Lambert C., *Le sepolture in urbe nella norma e nella prassi (tarda antichità-altomedioevo)*, in Paroli (ed.) 1997, pp.285-94.

La Rocca C., *"Dark Ages" a Verona: edilizia privata, aree aperte e strutture pubbliche in una città dell'Italia settentrionale*, "AM", XIII, 1986, pp.31-78.

La Rocca C., *Trasformazioni della città altomedievale in "Langobardia"*, "Studi Storici", 4, 1989, pp.993-1011.

La Rocca C., *Public buildings and urban change in northern Italy in the Early mediaeval period*, in J. Rich (ed.), *The city in Late Antiquity*, London-New York 1992, pp.161-80.

La Rocca C., *Una prudente maschera "antiqua". La politica edilizia di Teodorico*, Atti del XIII Congresso Internazionale di studi sull'alto medioevo (Milano 1992), 1993, Spoleto, pp.451-515.

La Rocca C., *"Castrum vel potius civitas". Modelli di declino urbano in Italia settentrionale durante l'altomedioevo*, in Francovich – Noyè (eds.) 1994, pp.545-54.

La Rocca C., *Segni di distinzione. Dai corredi funerari alle donazioni "post obitum" nel regno longobardo*, in Paroli (ed.), 1997, pp.31-54.

La Rocca C., *La Trasformazione del territorio in occidente*, Settimane di Studio…Spoleto 1998, pp.257-90.

La Rocca C., *Lo spazio urbano tra VI e VIII secolo*, Settimane di Studio…Spoleto 2003, pp.397-435.

Lavagna R., Varaldo C., *Osservazioni sui corredi funerari nella necropoli tardoantica e altomedievale del Priamàr a Savona, in Gelichi (ed.) 1997, pp.296-301.

Luni M., Ermeti A.L., Le mura di Urbino tra tardoantico e medioevo, in Gelichi (ed.) 1997, pp.41-50.

Lusuardi Siena S., Archeologia altomedievale a Luni: nuove scoperte nella basilica, "Quaderni del Centro di Studi Lunensi", I, 1976, pp.35-48.

Lusuardi Siena S., Ancora sulle torri "tarde" delle mura di Como, in Brogiolo (ed.), 1984, pp.67-77.

Lusuardi Siena S. (ed.), Ad Mensam, Manufatti d'uso da contesti archeologici tra Tarda Antichità e Medioevo, 1994, Udine.

Lusuardi Siena S., Alcune riflessioni sulla "ideologia funeraria" longobarda alla luce del recente scavo nella necropoli di S. Martino a Trezzo sull'Adda, in Paroli (ed.) 1997, pp.365-76.

Lusuardi Siena S., Sannazzaro M., Gli scavi della cattedrale di S. Maria, in Archeologia in Liguria II. Scavi e scoperte 1976-81, 1984, Genova, pp.36-48.

Lusuardi Siena S., Sannazzaro M., Area della cattedrale, in Archeologia in Liguria III.2. Scavi e scoperte 1982-86, Genova, 1987, pp.222-28.

Lusuardi Siena S., Giostra C., Spalla E., Sepolture e luoghi di culto in età longobarda: il modello regio, in Brogiolo (ed.) 2000, pp.273-83.

Maetzke G., La struttura stratigrafica dell'area nordoccidentale del Foro romano come appare dai recenti interventi di scavo, "AM", XVIII, 1991, pp.43-200.

Magrini C., Archeologia del paesaggio suburbano di Aquileia tra Tarda Antichità e Alto Medioevo, in Cuscito – Verzàr Bass 2004, pp.651-72.

Malnati L., Alluvioni e decadenza nella Modena tardo antica: alcune puntualizzazioni, "AM", XVII, 1990, pp.763-64.

Manacorda D., Marazzi F., Zanini E., Sul paesaggio urbano di Roma nell'Alto Medioevo, in Francovich – Noyè (eds.) 1994, pp.635-57.

Mannoni T., Vie e mezzi di comunicazione, "AM", X, 1983, pp.213-21.

Mannoni T., General remarks on the changes in techniques observable in the material culture of the first Millennium A.D. in North-West Italy, in Randsborg (ed.) 1989, pp.152-55.

Marazzi F., Le "città nuove" pontificie e l'insediamento laziale nel IX secolo, in Francovich – Noyé (eds.) 1994, pp.251-78.

Marazzi F., Da suburbium a territorium: il rapporto tra Roma e il suo hinterland nel paesaggio dall'antichità al medioevo, Settimane di Studio…Spoleto 2001, 713-51.

Melli P. (ed.), La città ritrovata. Archeologia urbana a Genova. 1984-1994, 1996, Genova.

MeneghiniSantangeli Valenzani, Sepolture intramuranee a Roma tra V e VII secolo d. C.Aggiornamenti e considerazioni, "AM", XXII, 1995, pp.283290.

Meneghini R., Santangeli Valenzani R., Episodi di trasformazione del paesaggio urbano nella Roma altomedievale attraverso l'analisi di due contesti: un isolato in piazza del Cinquecento e l'area dei Fori Imperiali, "AM", XXIII, 1996, pp.53-99.

Meneghini R., Roma. Strutture altomedievali e assetto urbano tra le regioni VII e VIII, "AM", XXVII, 2000, pp.303-10.

Meneghini R., L'origine di un quartiere altomedievale romano attraverso i recenti scavi del foro di Traiano, in Brogiolo (ed.) 2000, pp.55-59.

Mollo Mezzana R., La stratificazione archeologica di Augusta Praetoria, "Archeologia stratigrafica dell'Italia settentrionale", I, 1988, pp.74-100.

Munzi M., Ricci G., Serlorenzi M., Volterra tra tardo antico e alto medioevo, "AM", XXI, 1994, pp.639-56.

Negro Ponzi Mancini M., Problemi di tipologia e cronologia delle tombe altomedievali in Piemonte. Il caso di Trino (Vercelli), "Rivista di studi liguri", anno LIV, N.1-4, January-December 1988, pp.85-124.

Negro Ponzi Mancini M., Archeologia della produzione tra Tardo Antico e Altomedioevo, in Brogiolo (ed.) 1994, pp.53-65.

Negro Ponzi M., Romani, bizantini e longobardi: le fortificazioni tardo antiche e altomedievali nelle Alpi occidentali, in Brogiolo (ed.) 1999, pp.137-54.

Nepoti S., Dati sulla produzione medievale del vetro nell'area padana centrale, in Mendera J. (ed.), Archeologia e storia della produzione del vetro preindustriale, Firenze, 1991, pp.117-38.

Noyè G., Villes, èconomie et scietè dans la province de Bruttium-Lucanie du IV au VI siècle, in Francovich – Noyè (eds.) 1994, pp.693-733.

Noyè G., Les villes des provinces d'Apulie-Calabre et de Bruttium-Lucanie du IV au VI siècle, in Brogiolo (ed.) 1996, pp.97-120.

Orselli A.M., Coscienza e immagini della città nelle fonti tra V e IX secolo, in Brogiolo (ed.) 1996, pp.9-16.

Ortalli G., Venezia dalle origini a Pietro II Orseolo, in Delogu – Guillou – Ortalli (eds.), Longobardi e Bizantini, 1980, Torino, pp.339-428.

Ortalli G., La tecnica di costruzione delle strade di Bologna tra età romana e medioevo, "AM", XI, 1984, pp.379-94.

Ortalli G., L'edilizia abitativa, in A. Carile (ed.), Storia di Ravenna, vol. II, 1. Dall'età bizantina all'età ottoniana, 1991, Venezia, pp.167-92.

Ortalli G., Edilizia residenziale e crisi urbana nella tarda antichità: fonti archeologiche per la Cispadana, "XXXIX Corso di Cultura sull'arte Ravennate e Bizantina", 1992, Ravenna, pp.557-605.

Ortalli G., Nuove fonti archeologiche per "Ariminum": monumenti, opere pubbliche e assetto urbanistico…, in Calbi – Susini (eds.), Pro populo ariminense, Atti del Convegno, Faenza, 1995, pp.469-530.

Osborne J., Rasmus Brandt J., Moranti G. (eds.), Santa Maria Antiqua al Foro Romano: cento anni dopo, Atti del Colloquio Internazionale, Roma, 5-6 Maggio 2000, The British School at Rome, Rome, Campisano, 2005.

Panella C., Note conclusive, in Saguì (ed.) 1998, pp.815-22.

Panella C., Saguì L., *Consumo e produzione a Roma tra tardoantico e altomedioevo: le merci, i contesti*, Settimane di Studio...Spoleto 2001, pp.757-817.

Pani Ermini L., *Città fortificate e fortificazione delle città italiane fra V e VI secolo*, "Rivista di studi liguri", anno LIX-LX, January-December 1993-1994, pp.193-207.

Pani Ermini L., *La "città di pietra": forma, spazi, strutture*, Settimane di Studio...Spoleto 1998, pp.211-55.

Pani Ermini L., *Il recupero dell'altura nell'Alto Medioevo*, Settimane di Studio...Spoleto 1999, pp.613-64.

Pani Ermini L., Giuntella A.M., *Roma dal IV all'VIII secolo: quale paesaggio urbano?*, Ecole francaise de Rome, 1999.

Pani Ermini L., *Forma e cultura della città altomedievale: scritti scelti* (edited by A.M. Giuntella and M. Salvatore), Spoleto, 2001, pp.XII-488.

Pani Ermini L., *Forma Urbis: lo spazio urbano tra VI e IX secolo*, Settimane di Studio...Spoleto 2001, pp.255-323.

Parenti R., *Fonti materiali e lettura stratigrafica di un centro urbano: i risultati di una sperimentazione "non tradizionale"*, "AM", XIX, 1992, pp.7-62.

Parenti R., *I materiali da costruzione, le tecniche di lavorazione e gli attrezzi*, in Brogiolo (ed.) 1994, pp.25-37.

Paroli L., *Circolazione delle anfore globulari da trasporto e della ceramica invetriata nel mar Tirreno tra l'VIII e il X secolo*, in Brogiolo (ed.) 1996, pp.121-25.

Paroli L., Delogu P. (eds.), *La storia economica di Roma nell'alto medioevo alla luce dei recenti scavi archeologici*, Atti del Seminario (Roma 1992), 1993, Firenze.

Patitucci Uggeri S. (ed.), *Scavi medievali in Italia 1994-1995: atti della prima Conferenza italiana di archeologia medievale, Cassino (14-16 dicembre 1995)*, Roma 1998, "Quaderni di archeologia medievale"; "Supplemento I".

Patitucci Uggeri S. (ed.), *Scavi medievali in Italia 1996-1999: atti della seconda Conferenza italiana di archeologia medievale, Cassino 1999*, 2001.

Patitucci Uggeri S. (ed.), *La via Francigena e altre strade della Toscana medievale*, Firenze, 2004.

Pellecuer C., *Materiale di importazione di fine VII-prima metà VIII da San Peyre, sito rurale nell'entroterra di Languedoc...*, in Brogiolo (ed.) 1996, pp.126-32.

Pensabene P., *Monumenti medievali a Ferento nell'area del teatro e delle terme*, "Rivista di studi liguri", anno LIX-LX, January-December 1993-1994, pp.267-97.

Pergola Ph., *San Calocero d'Albenga: le sepolture tardo antiche ed alto medievali nell'ambito delle necropoli suburbane della città*, "Rivista di studi liguri", anno LIV, N.1-4, January-December 1988, 243-48.

Perinetti R., *Augusta Praetoria. Le necropoli cristiane*, Actes du XI Congrès International d'Archèologie Chrètienne (Lyon, 1986), Rome, 1989, pp.1215-226.

Pohl W., Wood I., Reimitz H., *The Transformation of Frontiers from late antiquity to the Carolingians*, Brill Academic Publishers, Amsterdam, 2001.

Quiròs Castillo J.A., *Architettura altomedievale lucchese*, "Archeologia dell'architettura", V, 2000, pp.131-54.

Randsborg K. (ed.), *The birth of Europe. Archaeological and social development in the first millennium A.D.*, 1989, Rome.

Rea R., *Roma: l'uso funerario della valle del Colosseo tra tardo antico e alto medioevo*, "AM", XX, 1993, pp.645-58.

Redi F., *Nuovi ritrovamenti archeologici a Palazzo Vitelli in Pisa*, "AM", IX, 1982, 416-17.

Redi F., *Pisa com'era: archeologia, urbanistica e strutture materiali (secoli V-XIV)*, 1991, Napoli.

Ricci M., *Relazioni culturali e scambi commerciali nell'Italia centrale romano-longobarda alla luce della Cripta Balbi in Roma*, in Paroli (ed.) 1997, pp.239-74.

Righini V., *Materiali e tecniche da costruzione in età tardo antica e alto medievale*, in A. Carile (ed.), *Storia di Ravenna*, vol. II, 1. *Dall'età bizantina all'età ottoniana*, 1991, Venezia, pp.193-221.

Ripoll G., Velazquez I., *Origen y desarrollo de las parrochiae en la Hispania de la antigua edad tarda*, in Pergola Ph., *Alle origini della parrocchia rurale (IV-VIII sec.)*, Atti della giornata tematica dei Seminari di Archeologia Cristiana, 1999, Città del Vaticano, pp.101-65.

Rossi F. (ed.), *Carta archeologica della Lombardia. V Brescia. La città*, I-II, 1996, Modena.

Rotili M., *Benevento romana e longobarda. L'immagine urbana*, 1986.

Saguì L. (ed.), *Ceramica in Italia: VI-VII secolo*, Firenze, 1998.

Saguì L., *Il deposito della Crypta Balbi: una testimonianza imprevedibile sulla Roma del VII secolo? Con Appendice di C. Capelli*, in Saguì (ed.) 1998, pp.305-34.

Santangeli Valenzani R., *Edilizia residenziale e aristocratica urbana a Roma nell'altomedioevo*, in Gelichi (ed.), Atti del I Congresso Nazionale di Archeologia Medievale, 1997, Pisa, pp.64-70.

Saxer V., *Le chiese rurali prima che fossero parrocchiali (IV-VIII sec.): proposte per una storia di quelle di Provenza*, in Pergola Ph., *Alle origini della parrocchia rurale (IV-VIII sec.)*, Atti della giornata tematica dei Seminari di Archeologia Cristiana, 1999, Città del Vaticano, pp.17-42.

Schmiedt G., *Città scomparse e città di nuova formazione in Italia in relazione al sistema di comunicazione*, XXI Settimana di Studio sull'alto medioevo (Spoleto 1973), 1974, Spoleto, pp.503-607.

Smith J.M.H., *Europe after Rome: a new cultural history 500-1000*, Oxford University Press, Oxford (UK), 2005.

Staffa A.R., *Scavi nel centro storico di Pescara, 1: primi elementi per una ricostruzione dell'assetto antico ed alto medievale dell'abitato di "Ostia Aeterni-Aternum"*, "AM", XVIII, 1991, pp.201-378.

Staffa A.R., *Forme di abitato alto medievale in Abruzzo. Un approccio etnoarcheologico*, in Brogiolo (ed.) 1994, pp.67-88.

Staffa A.R., *Una terra di frontiera: Abruzzo e Molise fra VI e VII secolo*, in Brogiolo (ed.) 1995, pp.187-238.

Staffa A.R., *I Longobardi in Abruzzo (secc. VI-VII)*, in Paroli (ed.) 1997, pp.113-66.

Staffa A.R., *La città altomedievale: esempi dall'Abruzzo*, in Gelichi (ed.) 1997, pp.71-74.

Staffa A.R., *Le produzioni ceramiche in Abruzzo tra fine V e VII secolo*, in Saguì (ed.) 1998, pp.437-80.

Tabacco G., *La città vescovile nell'Alto Medioevo*, in P. Rossi (ed.), *Modelli di città. Strutture e funzioni politiche*, 1987, Torino, pp.267-345.

Tabacco G., *Egemonie sociali e strutture del potere nel medioevo italiano*, 1992.

Testini P., Cantino Wataghin G., Pani Ermini L., *La cattedrale in Italia*, Actes du XI Congrès International d'Archèologie Chrètienne (Lyon, Vienne, Grenoble, Genève et Aoste 1986), 1989, Rome, pp.5-229.

Tirelli M., *Altino, frontiera lagunare bizantina: le testimonianze archeologiche*, in Brogiolo (ed.) 1995, pp.115-20.

Tiussi C., *Il sistema di distribuzione di Aquileia: mercati e magazzini*, in Cuscito – Verzàr Bass (eds.) 2004, pp.257-316.

Tortorella S., *La sigillata in Italia nel VI e nel VII secolo d. C.: problemi di cronologia e distribuzione*, in Saguì (ed.) 1998, pp.42-70.

Valenti M., Fronza V., *Un archivio per l'edilizia in materiale deperibile nell'altomedioevo*, in M. Valenti (ed.), *Poggio imperiale a Poggibonsi: dal villaggio di capanne al castello di pietra. 1. Diagnostica archeologica e campagne di scavo 1991-94*, 1996, Firenze, pp.159-218.

Van de Noort R., *The archaeology of Dark Ages...*, "AM", XIX, 1992, pp.487-90.

Vannini G., *Un problema topografico alle origini di Firenze comunale*, in Ciardi Dupré Dal Poggetto M.G., Dal Poggetto P. (eds.), *Scritti di storia dell'arte in onore di Ugo Procacci*, vol. I, Milano, 1977, pp.51-61.

Vannini G. (ed.), *L'antico Palazzo dei Vescovi a Pistoia*, 1985.

Vannini G., *Pistoia altomedievale*, in *Pistoia e la Toscana nel Medioevo. Studi per Natale Rauty*, Biblioteca Storica Pistoiese, vol. I, 1997, pp.37-54.

Vannini G., *Florentia altomedievale: le mura carolingie, storia e topografia di un mito di fondazione, Metodologia, insediamenti urbani e produzioni. Il contributo di Gabriella Maetzke e le attuali prospettive delle ricerche*, Convegno Internazionale di studi sull'Archeologia Medievale in memoria di Gabriella Maetzke Viterbo, November 2004, publishing in progress.

Villa L., *Aquileia tra Goti, Bizantini e Longobardi: spunti per un'analisi delle trasformazioni urbane nella transizione fra Tarda Antichità e Alto Medioevo*, in Cuscito – Verzàr Bass (eds.) 2004, pp.561-632.

Violante C., Fonseca C.D., *Ubicazione e dedicazione delle cattedrali dalle origini al periodo romanico nelle città dell'Italia centrosettentrionale*, in *Il romanico pistoiese nei suoi rapporti con l'arte romanica dell'Occidente*, Atti del I Convegno Internazionale di Studi Medioevali di Storia e D'Arte ( Pistoia 1964), 1969, Pistoia, pp.303-46.

Visser Travagli A.M., *Archeologia urbana a Ferrara*, "Archeologia stratigrafica in Italia settentrionale", 1, 1988, pp.133-41.

Ward Perkins B., *Archeologia altomedievale a Luni: gli insediamenti*, "Quaderni del Centro di Studi Lunense", 1, 1976, pp.27-34.

Ward Perkins B., *Lo scavo nella zona nord del Foro. Sepolture e pozzi d'acqua*, in *Scavi di Luni*, vol. II, 1977, Roma, pp.633-38, 664-71.

Ward Perkins B., *L'abbandono degli edifici pubblici a Luni*, "Quaderni del Centro di Studi Lunense", 3, 1978, pp.33-46.

Ward Perkins B., *La città altomedievale*, "AM", X, 1983, pp.111-24.

Ward Perkins B., *From classical Antiquity to the Middle Ages. Urban public building in northern and central Italy, AD 300-850*, 1984, Oxford.

Ward Perkins B., *The towns of northern Italy: rebirth or reneval?*, in Hodges – Hobley (eds.) 1988, pp.16-27.

Ward Perkins B., *Urban Continuity?*, in Christie – Loseby (eds.) 1996, pp.4-17.

Whitehouse D., Michaelides D., *Scavi di emergenza ad Otranto*, "AM", VI, 1979, pp.269-70.

Whittaker C.R., *Trade and the Aristocracy in the Roman Empire*, "Opus", 4, 1985, pp.49-75.

Wickham C., *Early medieval Italy. Central power and local society 400-1000*, 1981, London.

Wickham C., *L'Italia e l'altomedioevo*, "AM", XV, 1988, pp.105-24.

Wickham C., *La città altomedievale. Una nota sul dibattito in corso*, "AM", XV, 1988, pp.649-51.

Wickham C., *Considerazioni conclusive*, in Francovich – Noyè (eds.) 1994, pp.741-59.

Wickham C., *Early medieval archaeology in Italy: the last twenty years*, "AM", XXVI, 1999, pp.7-20.

Wickham C., *Framing the Early Middle Ages: Europe and the Mediterranean, 400-800*, Oxford University Press, Oxford (UK), 2005.

# Index of nouns (authors, places, technical and specific terms)*

Abbreviations.

Introduction: Intr.; Chapter: Ch.; Conclusions: Con.; Page: P.; Note: N.

---

* Some nouns are intentionally omitted as they are found throughout the whole text and/or they are constantly the topic of this work (Byzantine; Late Antiquity; Longobard/Lombard; Roman; [Early] Middle Ages); on the other hand, such an omission is not applied to the noun "Italy", in order to distinguish the different geographical areas of the peninsula specifically mentioned.

## Appendix I. List of Roman Emperors (from the end of the second century AD).

**Severan dynasty.**
*Pertinax* (193).
*Didius Julianus* (193).
*Septimius Severus* (193-211).
[claimants during his reign: *Pescennius Niger*, Emperor in Syria (193-194/95; *Clodius Albinus*, Emperor in Britain (193/95-197)].
*Geta* (209December 211)
*Caracalla* (February 211-17).
*Macrinus* (217-18) and *Diadumenian* (217-18).
*Elagabalus* (218-22).
*Alexander Severus* (222-35).

**Emperors during the so-called Military Anarchy (235-84).**
*Maximinus* Thrax (235-38).
Gordian I (238).
Gordian II (238).
*Pupienus Maximus* (238).
*Balbinus* (238).
Gordian III (238-44).
[during his reign *Sabinianus* (240) proclaimed himself emperor].
Philip the Arab (244-49).
[during his reign claimants: *Pacatianus* (248); *Iotapianus* and the usurper: *Silbannacus* (248)].
*Decius* (249-51).
[during and soon after his reign claimants: *Priscus* (249-52), emperor in the Eastern provinces; *Licinianus* (250)].
*Herennius Etruscus* (251).
*Hostilian* (251), *Trebonianus Gallus* (251-53) and *Volusianus* (251-53).
*Aemilianus* (253).
Valerian (253-60), *Gallienus* (253-68), *Saloninus* (260) and *Postumus* (260-69).
[during their reign one claimant: *Quietus* (260-61) and several leaders who proclaimed themselves emperor: *Ingenuus* (258 or 260); *Regalianus* (260); *Macrianus Major* (260-61); *Mussius Aemilianus* (261-61/62); *Aureolus* (268); *Laelianus* in the Gallic Province/Empire (269)].
*Marius* (269).
*Victorinus* (269-71).
[*Domitianus* proclaimed himself emperor of the Gallic Empire (270-71)].
*Tetricus* (271-74).

**Illyrian Emperors.**
*Claudius II Gothicus* (268-70).
*Quintillus* (270).
Aurelian (270-75).
[during his reign *Septimius* proclaimed himself emperor in *Dalmatia* (271)].
*Tacitus* (275-76).

*Florianus* (276).
*Probus* (276-82).
[during his reign claimants: *Saturninus* (280); *Proculus* (280) while *Bonosus* proclaimed himself emperor (280)].
*Carus* (282-83).
*Carinus* (283-85) and Numerian (283-84).

**Tetrarchic-Age Emperors.**
Diocletian (284-305) and Maximian (286-305).
[but in Britain: *Carausius* (286-93; *Allectus* (293-97)].
*Constantius I Chlorus* (305-06), *Galerius* (305-11), *Severus II* (306-07), *Maxentius* (306-12) and Maximian (307-08).

**Constantinian dynasty.**
Constantine I the Great (307/09-37), *Licinius* (308-24), *Maximinus Daia* (310-13), *Valerius Valens* (316-17) and *Martinianus* (324).
[*Domitius Alexander* proclaimed himself emperor (308)].
Constantine II (337-40), *Constantius II* (337-61), *Constans* (337-50) and *Vetranio* (350).
[during this time the usurper *Magnentius* (350-53); while *Nepotianus* proclaimed himself emperor (350).
Julian (361-63).
Jovian (363-64).

**Valentinian and Theodosian dynasties.**
Valentinian I (364-75), in the West.
*Valens* (364-78), in the East.
[during his reign the usurper *Procopius* (365-66)].
Gratian (367-83).
Valentinian II (375-92).
*Theodosius* I (379-95).
*Magnus Maximus* (383-88) and his son *Flavius* Victor (386-88).
*Arcadius* (383-95), by AD 395 only in the East.
*Honorius* (393-95), by AD 395 only in the West.

**Western Empire.**
*Honorius* (395-423) and *Constantius III* (421).
[several claimants: Constantine III (407-11); *Constans II* (409-11); *Maximus* (409-11), ruled on *Hispania*; *Jovinus* (411-13); *Sebastianus* (412-413); while *Priscus Attalus* was proclaimed emperor by the Visigoths (409-10 and 414-15).
*Joannes*, claimant (423-25).
Valentinian III (425-55).
*Petronius Maximus* (455).
*Avitus* (455-56).
Majorian (457-61).
*Libius Severus* (461-65).
*Anthemius* (467-72).
*Olybrius* (472).
*Glycerius* (473-74).

*Julius Nepos* (474-75 and 476-80, deposed by *Orestes* in 475 but finally recognised by Odoacer).
*Romulus Augustus* (475-76), deposed by Odoacer.

**Eastern Empire.**
*Arcadius* (395-408).
*Theodosius* II (408-50).
Marcian (450-57).
Leo I (457-74).
Leo II (474).
*Zeno* (474-91) and *Basiliscus* (475-76).

## Appendix II. Kings and Rulers in Late-Antiquity and Early-Middle-Ages Italy.

**Ostrogothic Kingdom.**
Theodoric the Great (476/89-526).
Amalasuntha for Athalaric (526-34).
*Theodahad* (534-36).
*Vitige* (also *Witiges*; 536-40).
*Ildibad* (540-41).
*Eraric* (541).
*Baduela* (also known as *Totila* [immortal]; 541-52).
*Theia* (also *Teian, Teia*; 552-53).

**Longobard Kingdom.**
Alboin (568-72).
Cleph (572-74).
Ten Year *Interregnum* (574-84).
*Authari* (584-90).
Agilulf (591-616).
Adaloald (616-26).
Arioald (626-36).
*Rothari* (636-52).
Rodoald (652-53).
Aripert I (653-661).
Perctarit (also *Berthari*) and Godepert (661-62).
Grimoald (also Grimuald, 662-71). [Garibald (669)].
Perctarit (671-688), restore from exile.
*Alahis* (688-89), rebel duke of *Friuli*.
Cunincpert (also Cunipert; 688-700).
Liutpert (700-01).
Raginpert (701).
Aripert II (701-12).
Ansprand (712).
Liutprand (712-44).
Hildeprand (744).
*Ratchis* (744-49).
Aistulf (749-56).
*Desiderius* (756-74).

**Frankish Kingdom.**
Charles I the Great (Charlemagne; 771-81).
Pippin (781-810).
Bernard (810-18).
Lothair I (818-39).
Louis II the German (839-75).
Charles II the Bald (875-77).
Carloman (877-79).
Charles III the Fat (879-87).
Berengar I (888-924; emperor from 915).

Several claimants during Berengar's reign:
Guy (889-94).
Lambert (892-98).
Arnulf (896-99).
Louis III the Blind (900-05).
Rudolph (922-33).
Hugh of Provence (924-47).
Lothair II (947-50).
Berengar II (950-61) and Adalbert (950-63).

**The Kingdom of Italy, subjected to Otto I, became part of the Holy Roman Empire in 955.**

Otto I (962-73).
Otto II (973-83).
Otto III (983-1002).
Arduin (1002-14).
Henry II (1004-24).
Conrad II (1026-39).
Henry III (1039-56).
Henry IV (1080-93).
Conrad (1093-98).
Henry V (1099-1125).

# Appendix III. List of Popes (third to eleventh century AD).

*Zephyrinus* (199-217).
*Callistus I* (217-22).
Urban I (222-30).
Pontain (230-35).
*Anterus* (235-36).
Fabian (236-50).
*Cornelius* (251-53).
*Lucius I* (253-54).
Stephen I (254-57).
*Sixtus II* (257-58).
*Dionysius* (260-68).
Felix I (269-74).
Eutychian (275-83).
*Caius* (also *Gaius*, 283-96).
*Marcellinus* (296-304).
*Marcellus* I (308-09).
*Eusebius* (309/310).
*Miltiades* (311-14).

**Edict of Milan (313).**

-Sylvester (314-35).
*Marcus* (336).
*Julius I* (337-52).
*Liberius* (352-66).
*Damasus* (366-83).
*Siricius* (384-99).
*Anastasius I* (399-401).
Innocent I (401-17).
*Zosimus* (417-18).
Boniface I (418-22).
Celestine I (422-32).
*Sixtus III* (432-40).
Leo I the Great (440-61).
*Hilarius* (461-68).
*Simplicius* (468-83).
Felix III (II) (483-92).
*Gelasius I* (492-96).
*Anastasius II* (496-98).
*Symmachus* (498-514).
*Hormisdas* (514-23).
John I (523-26).
Felix IV (III) (526-30).
Boniface II (530-32).
John II (533-35).
*Agapetus I* (also *Agapitus*, 535-36).
*Silverius* (536-37).
*Vigilius* (537-55).
*Pelagius I* (556-61).
John III (561-74).
Benedict I (575-79).
*Pelagius II* (579-90).
Gregory I the Great (590-604).
Sabinian (604-06).
Boniface III (607).

Boniface IV (608-15).
*Deusdedit* (also *Adeodatus I*, 615-18).
Boniface V (619-25).
*Honorius I* (625-38).
*Severinus* (640).
John IV (640-42).
Theodore I (642-49).
Martin I (649-55).
Eugene I (655-57).
Vitalian (657-72).
*Adeodatus II* (672-76).
*Donus* (676-78).
Agatho (678-81).
Leo II (682-83).
Benedict II (684-85).
John V (685-86).
Conon (686-87).
*Sergius I* (687-701).
John VI (701-05).
John VII (705-07).
*Sisinnius* (708).
Constantine (708-15).
Gregory II (715-31).
Gregory III (731-41).
Zachary (741-52).
Stephen II (752) [sometimes omitted because he died
          before being consecrated].
Stephen III (II) (752-57).
Paul I (757-67).
Stephen IV (767-72).
Adrian I (772-95).
Leo III (795-816).
Stephen V (816-17).
Paschal I (817-24).
Eugene II (824-27).
Valentine (827).
Gregory IV (827-44).
*Sergius II* (844-47).
Leo IV (847-55).
Benedict III (855-58).
Nicholas I the Great (858-67).
Adrian II (867-72).
John VIII (872-82).
*Marinus I* (882-84).
Adrian III (884-85).
Stephen VI (885-91).
*Formosus* (891-96).
Boniface VI (896).
Stephen VII (896-97).
*Romanus* (897).
Theodore II (897).
John IX (898-900).
Benedict IV (900-03).
Leo V (903).
*Sergius III* (904-11).

*Anastasius III* (911-13).
*Lando* (913-14).
John X (914-28).
Leo VI (928).
Stephen VIII (929-31).
John XI (931-35).
Leo VII (936-39).
Stephen IX (939-42).
*Marinus II* (942-46).
*Agapetus II* (946-55).
John XII (955-63).
Leo VIII (963-64).
Benedict V (964).
John XIII (965-72).
Benedict VI (973-74).
Benedict VII (974-83).
John XIV (983-84).
John XV (985-96).
Gregory V (996-99).
Sylvester II (999-1003).
John XVII (1003).

John XVIII (1003-09).
*Sergius IV* (1009-12).
Benedict VIII (1012-24).
John XIX (1024-32).
Benedict IX (1032-45) [twice removed and restored; see below].
Sylvester III (1045) [antipope?].
Benedict IX (1045).
Gregory VI (1045-46).
Clement II (1046-47).
Benedict IX (1047-48).
*Damasus II* (1048).
Leo IX (1049-54).
Victor II (1055-57).
Stephen X (1057-58).
Nicholas II (1058-61).
Alexander II (1061-73).
Gregory VII (1073-85).
Victor III (1086-87).
Urban II (1088-99).
Paschal II (1099-1118).

**Fig. 1a.** African *sigillata* (Red Slip Ware) distribution over the Italian peninsula: AD 450-570/80. Types C and D (triangle); Type D only (circle); unpublished sites (asterix). (After Tortorella 1998).

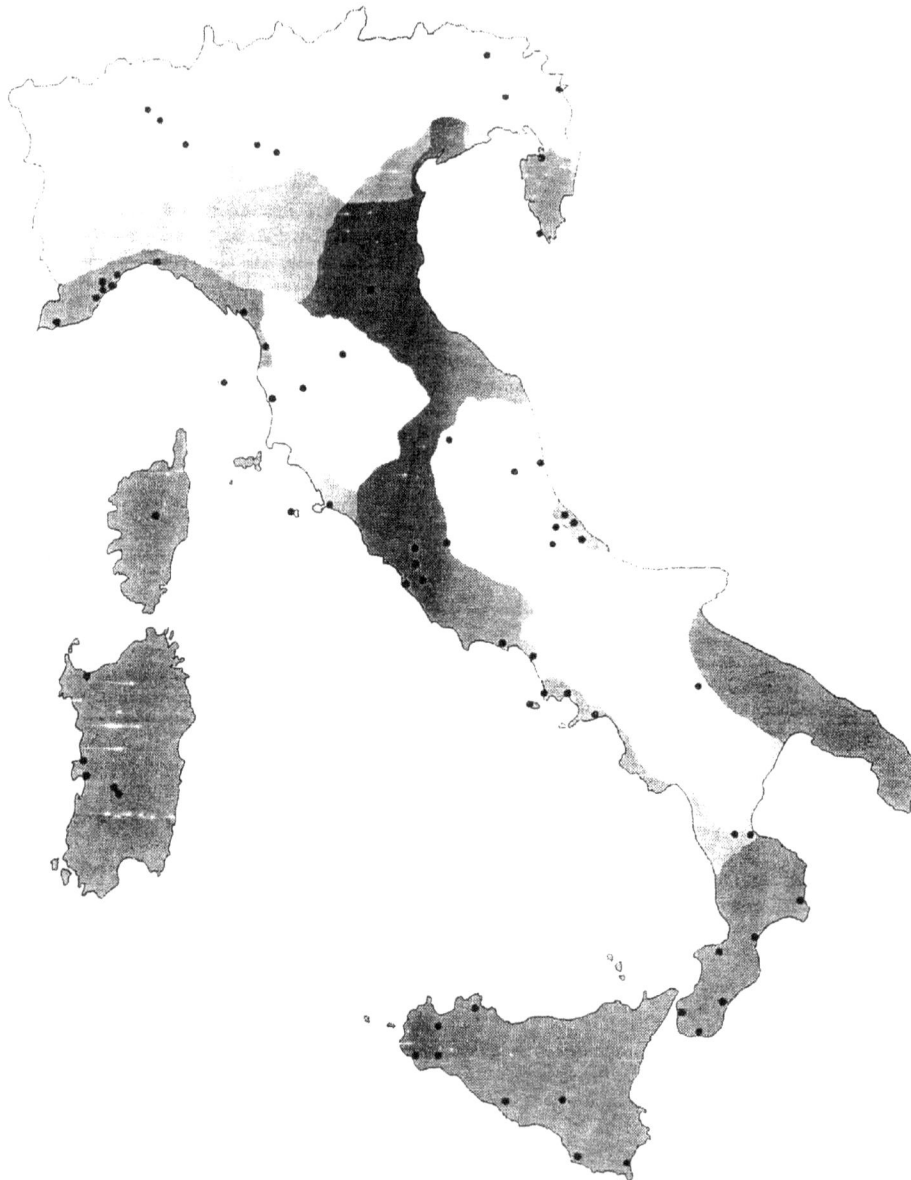

**Fig. 1b. African *sigillata* (Red Slip Ware) distribution: AD 550-seventh century. Longobard territory (white); territories conquered by Longobards in the span AD 585-c. 610 (light grey); territories under *Byzantium* in the early seventh century (dark grey). (After Tortorella 1998).**

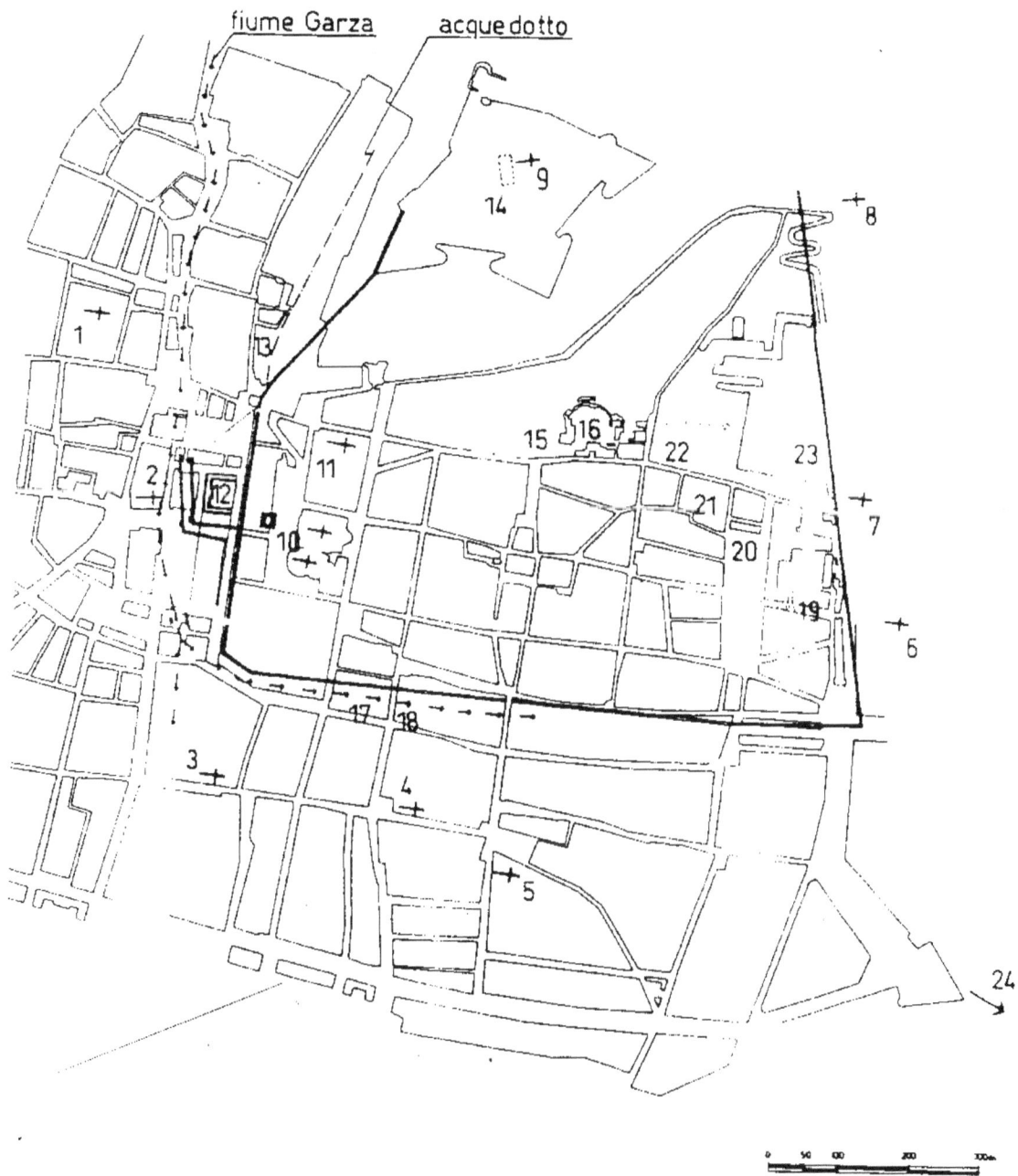

Fig. 2. *Brescia*. Map of the Late-Antique town (fourth to mid-sixth century). Buildings and areas mentioned in the text: 3. *St. Alessandro*; 5. *St. Faustino ad sanguinem*; 10. Episcopal Complex: *St. Pietro* and *St. Maria*'s Cathedral, Baptistery of *St. Giovanni*; 12. Palace (the so-called "winged edifice"); 15. *Capitolium/Pallaveri* House; 19. *Via Alberto Mario* (Street); 22. *St. Giulia* (*St. Salvatore*); 23. *Ortaglia* (Quarter); 24. *Via Mantova* (Street) towards the port. Ruler: 0 – 330 yd./300 m. (After Brogiolo 1993).

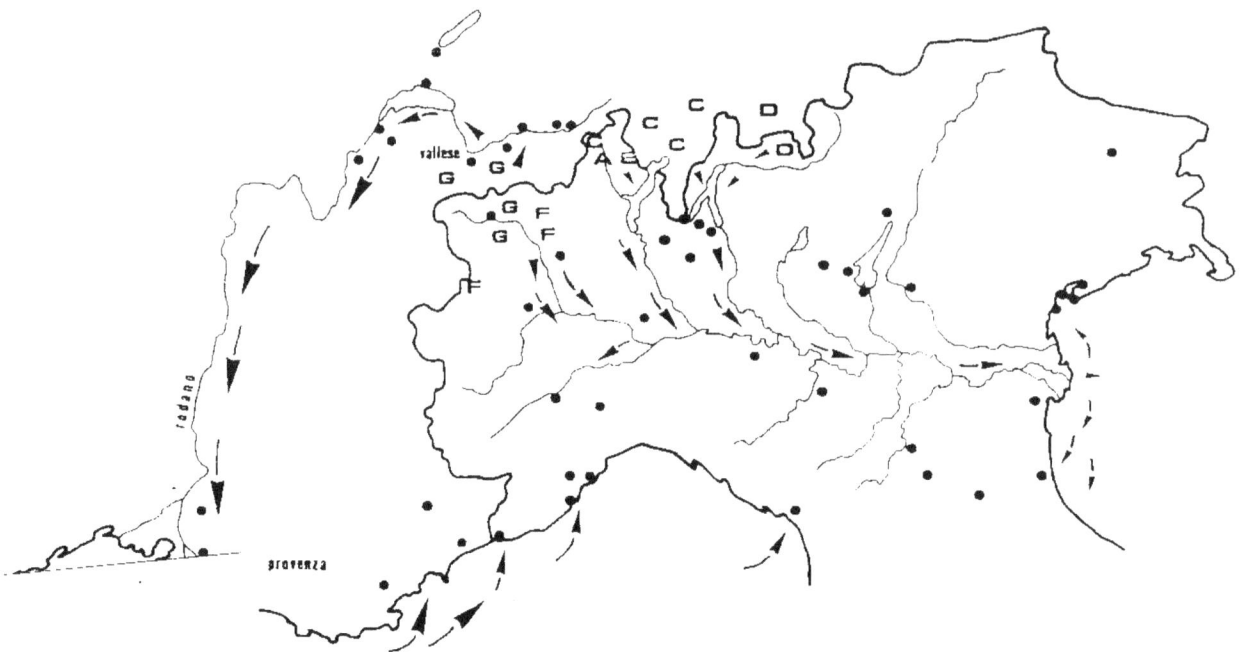

**Fig. 3. Eventual watercourses used for soapstone-dolomite trading over North Italy. The main sites along the _Rhone_ (_Rodano_) and over the _Po_ Valley where importations of the kind have been found out are marked with a full circle. (After Alberti 1997).**

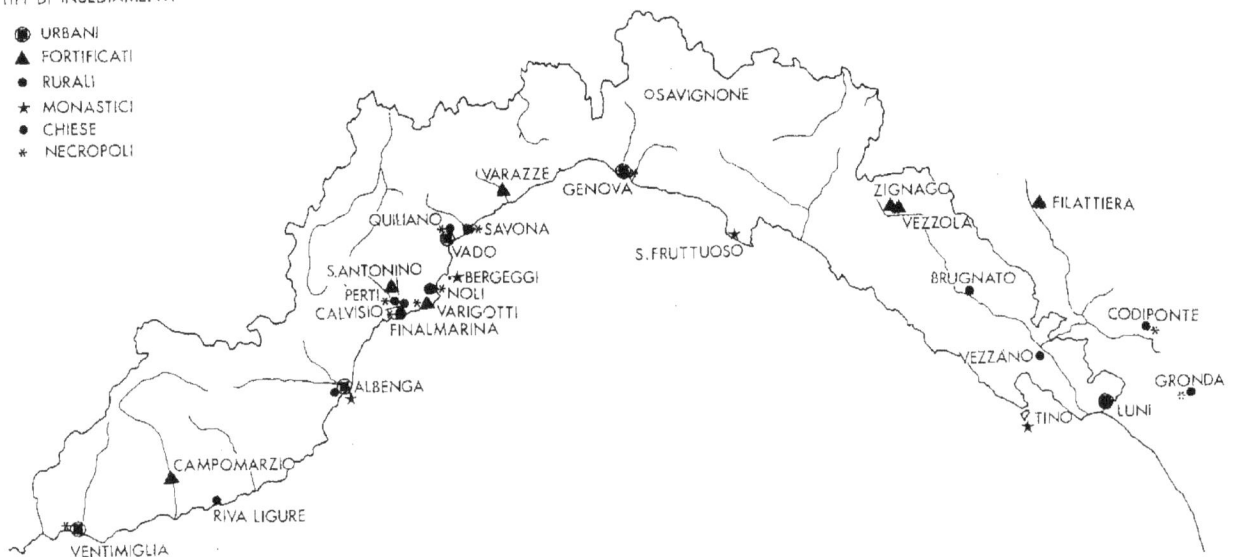

**Fig. 4. Region _Liguria_ map (displaying site-category; _chiese_=churches). (After Gardini – Murialdo 1994).**

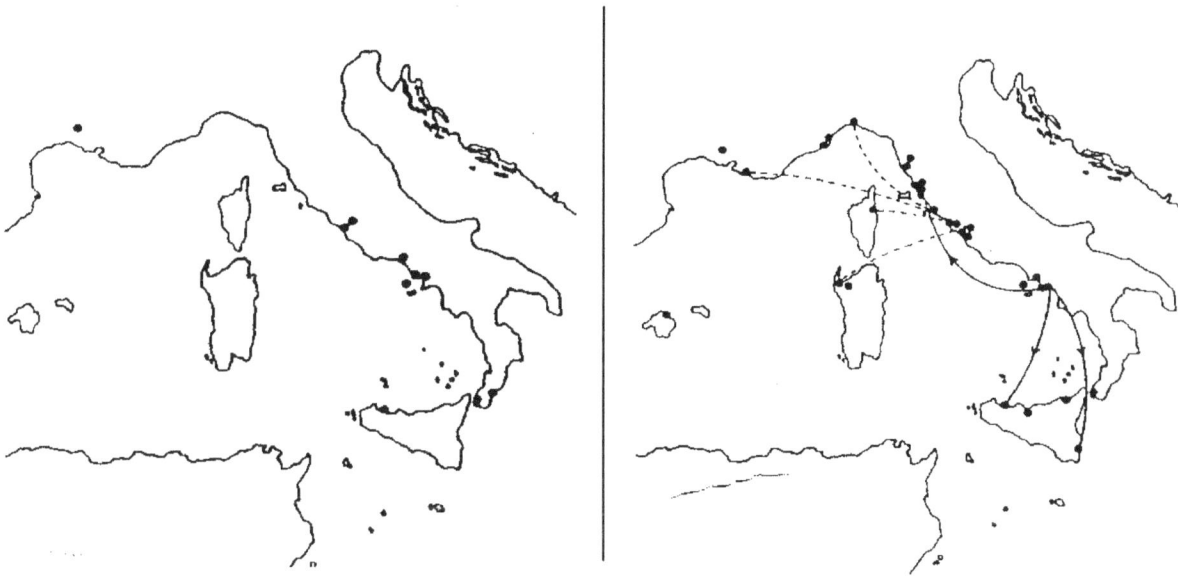

**Fig. 5a (left). Distribution map of late seventh-eighth century "globular" *amphorae*. (After Paroli 1996).**

**Fig. 5b. Map of western coast-sites with finds of Early Medieval glazed pottery. (After Paroli 1996).**

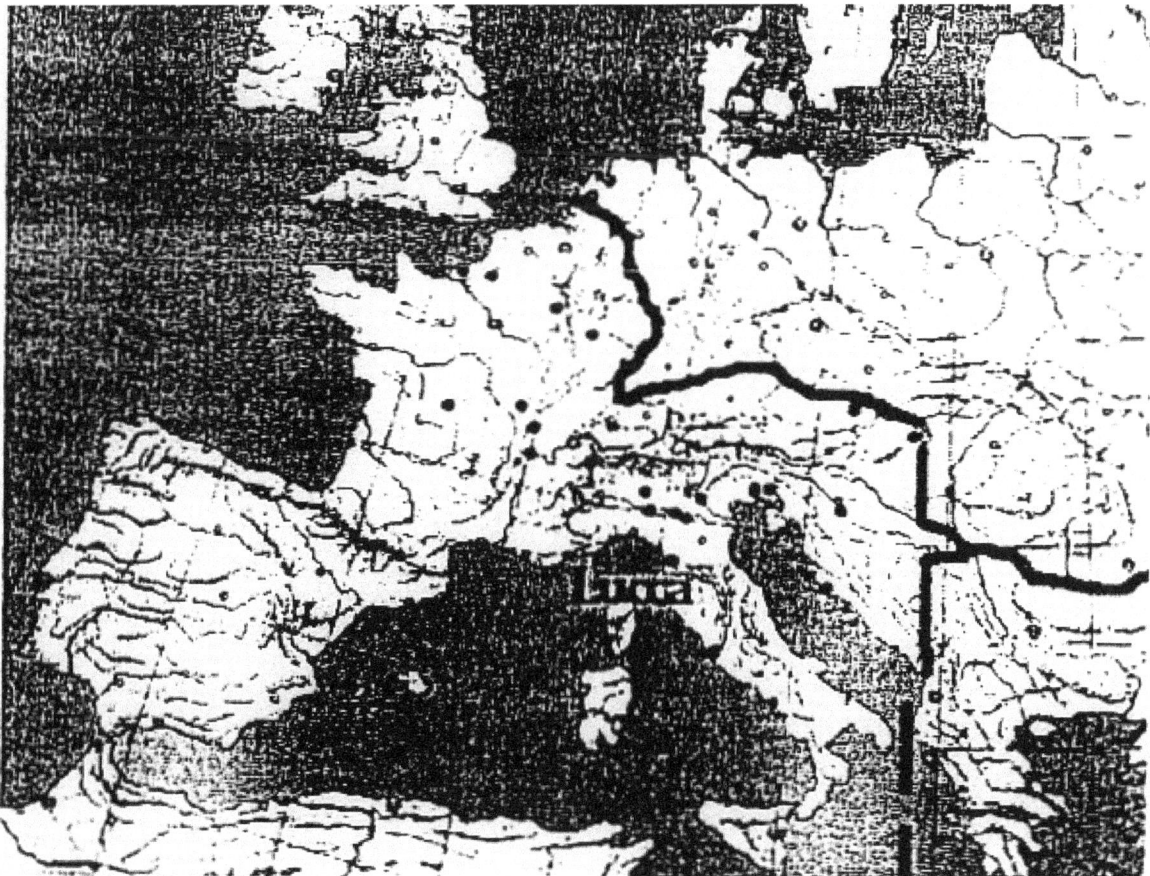

**Fig. 6. Map of Late Antique *fabricae* (factories) in the *pars occidentalis* (western areas) according to the *Notitia Dignitatum*. (After Citter 1998).**

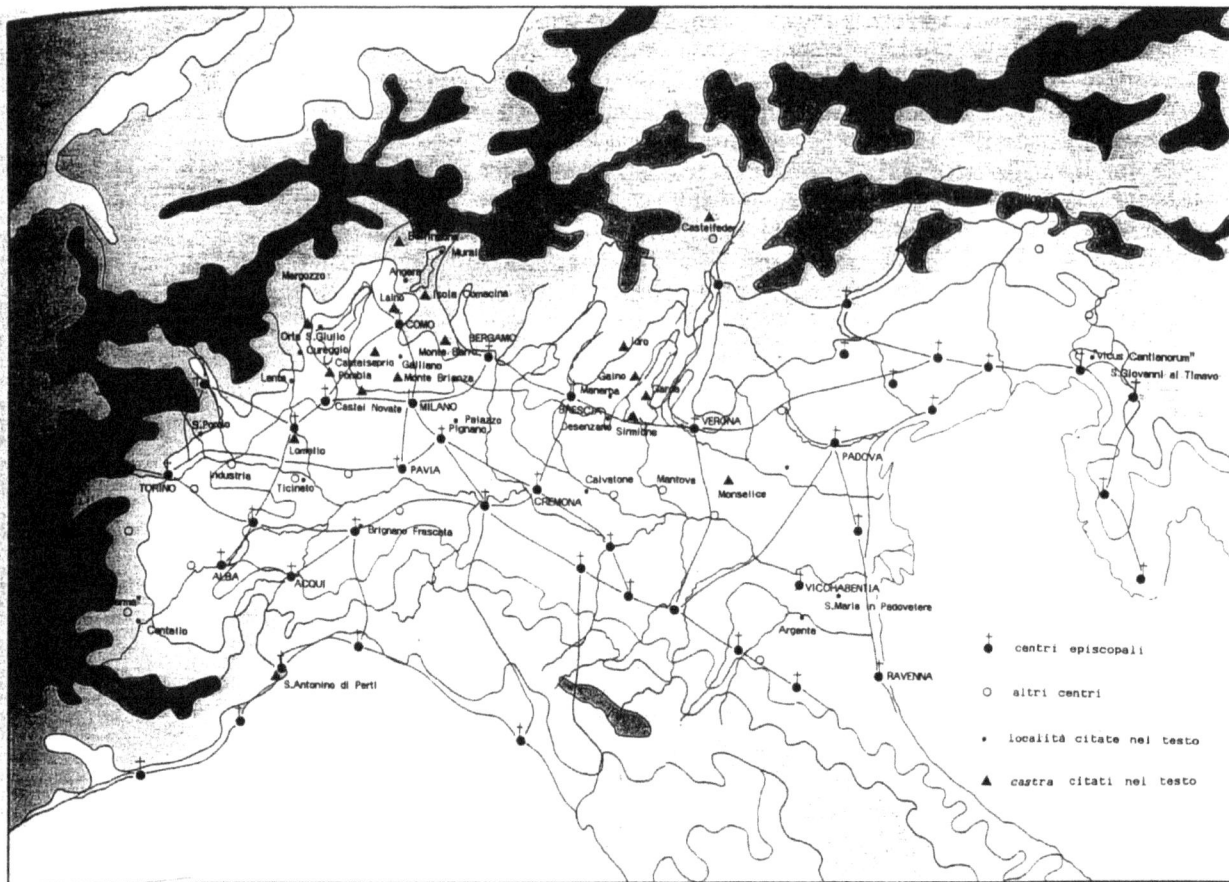

**Fig. 7. Map of North Italy with some important *castra* (triangle), towns (small and empty circle) and episcopal centres (full circle with a cross). (After Cantino Wataghin 1994).**

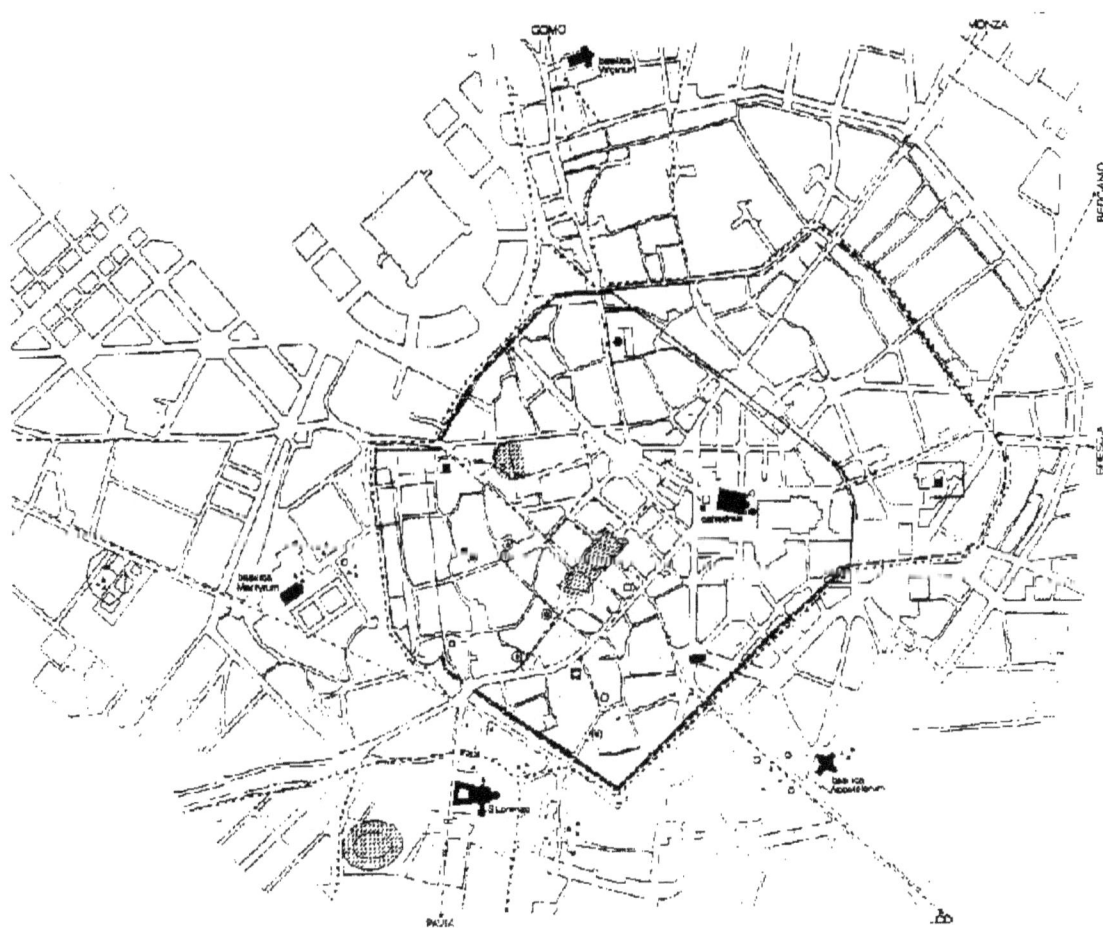

**Fig. 8. Milan. Map of the Late Antique city (cathedral=black building inside the circle of walls).
(After Testini et alii 1989).**

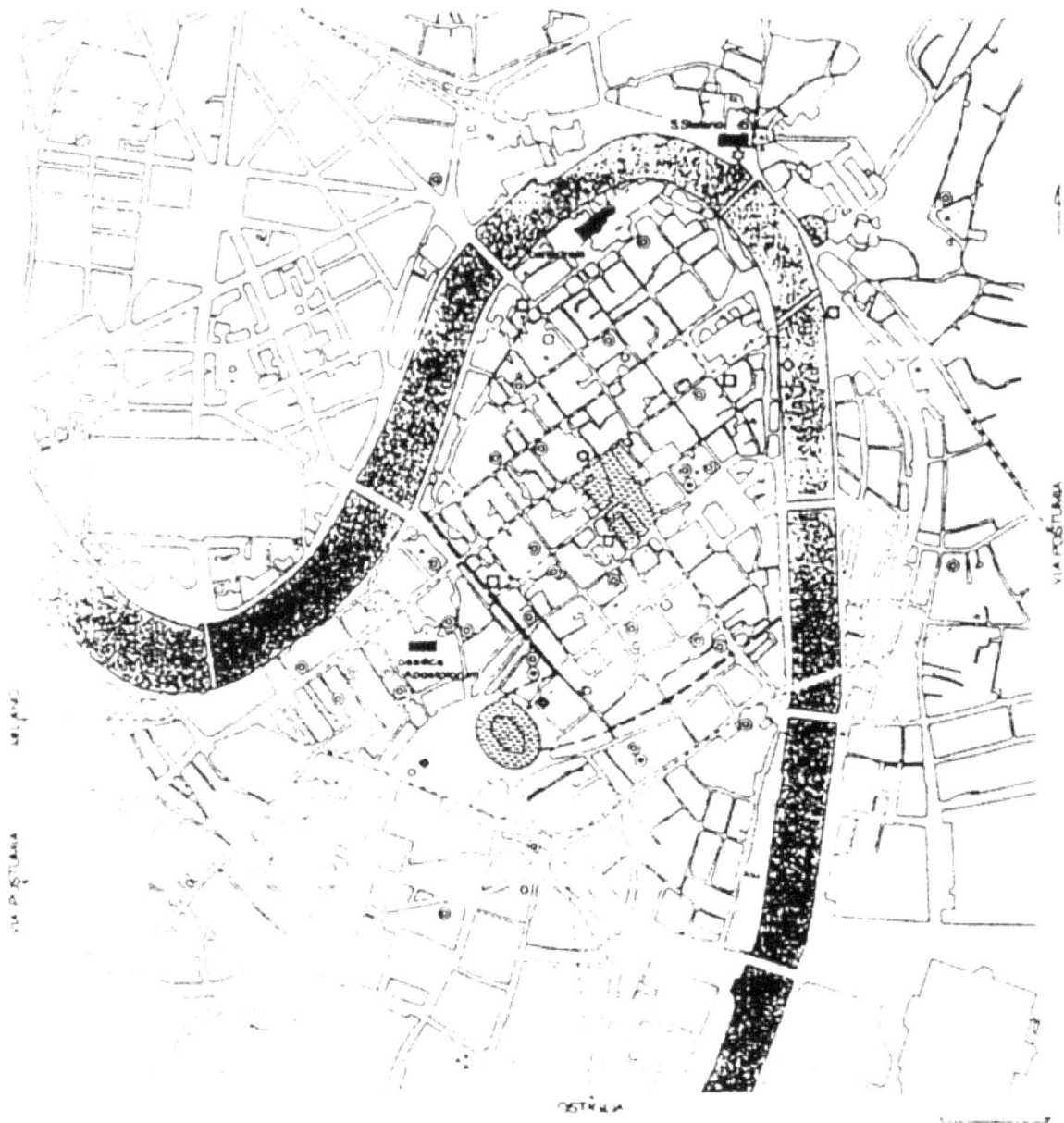

Fig. 9a. *Verona*. Map of the town. (After Cantino Wataghin – Lambert 1998).

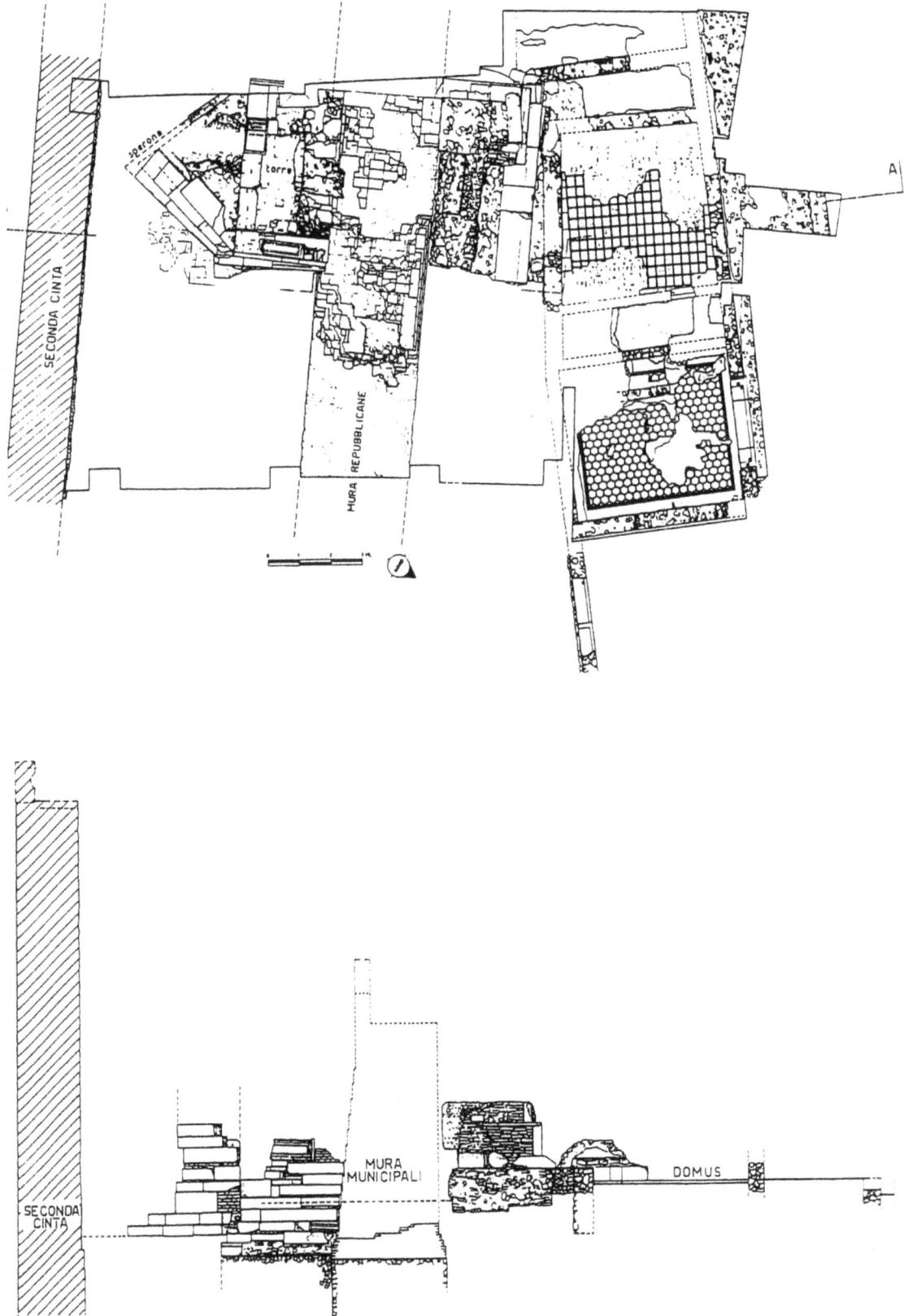

**Fig. 9b.** *Verona, via St. Cosimo* (Street) 3. **Plan and cross-section of the surveyed site; particularly noteworthy the Republican-Age fortifications, the 5th-century buttresses and the enlargement of walls ascribed to the epoch of** *Theodoric* (*cinta*=circle of walls; *torre*=tower; *mura repubblicane*=Republican-Age walls; *mura municipali*=city-walls). **(After Cavalieri Manasse 1993).**

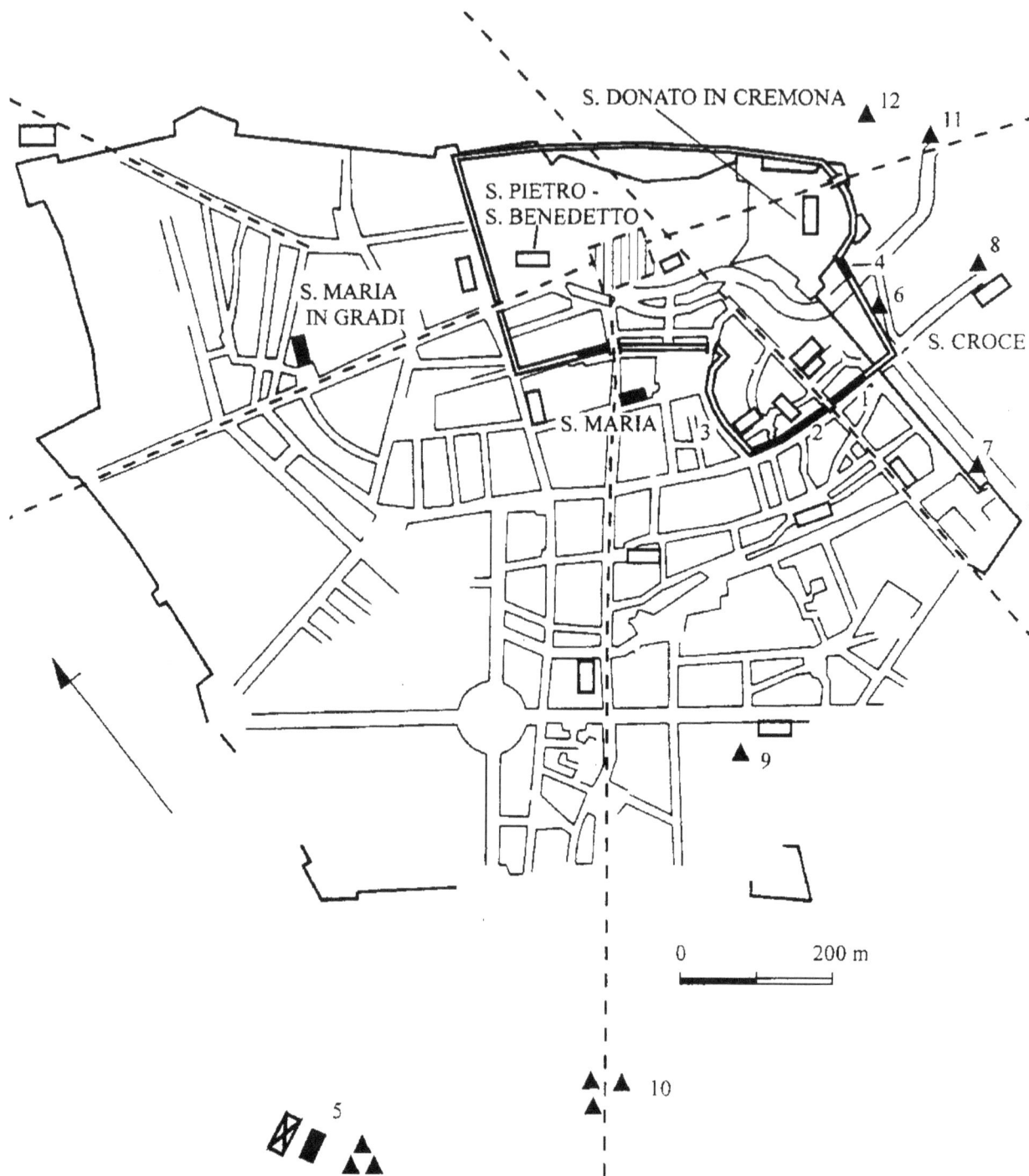

**Fig. 10 (see also fig.24). Late Antique and Early Medieval *Arezzo*. Ruler: 0 – 220 yd./200 m. (After Gelichi 1999).**

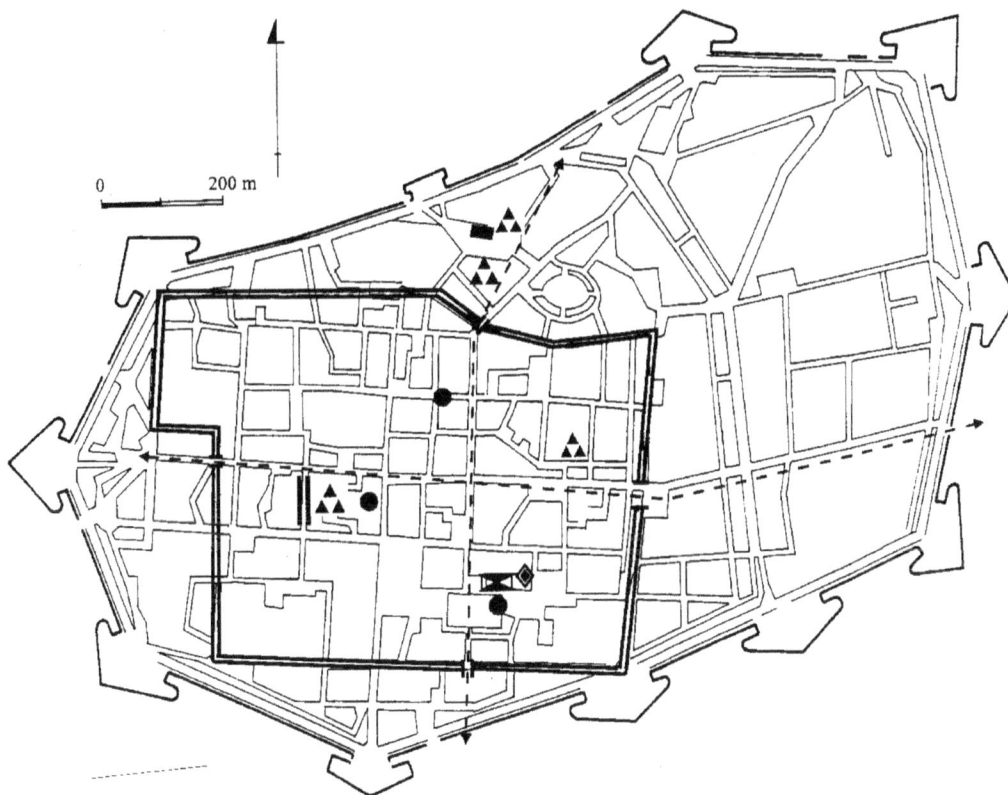

**Fig. 11a (see also fig.24). Late Antique *Lucca*. Ruler: 0 – 220yd./200 m. (After Gelichi 1999).**

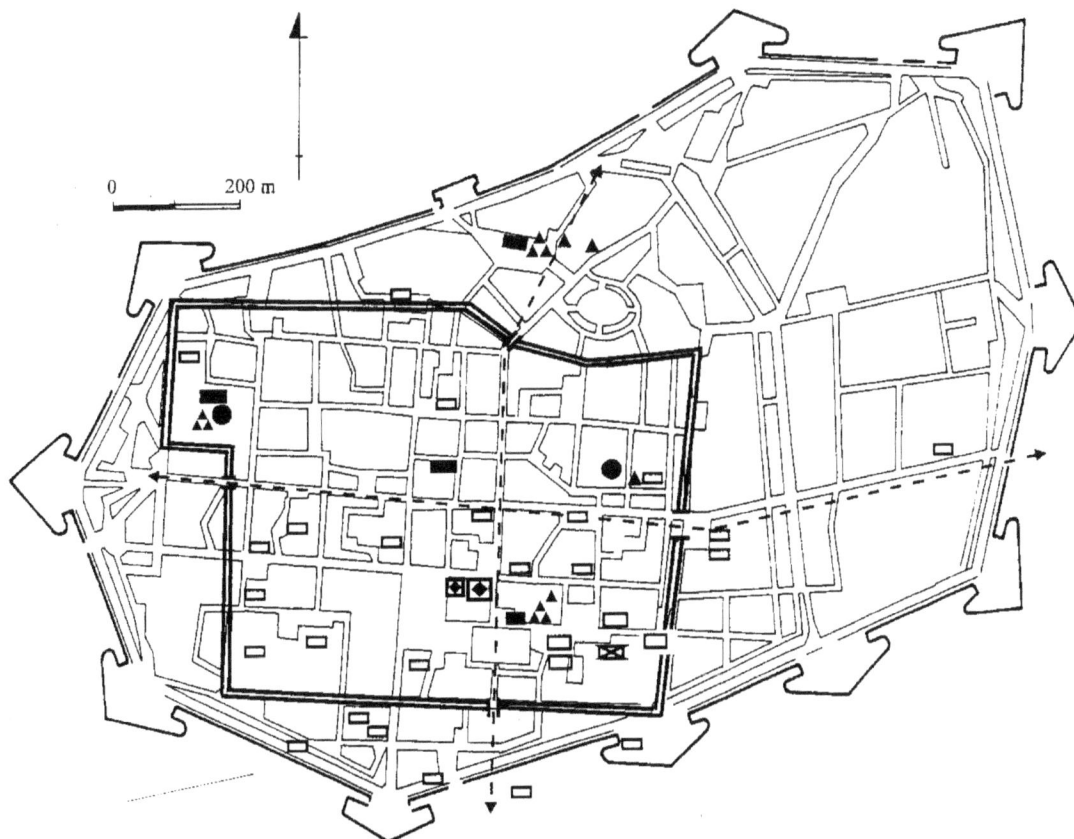

**Fig. 11b (see also fig.24). Early Medieval *Lucca*. Ruler: 0 – 220yd./200 m. (After Gelichi 1999).**

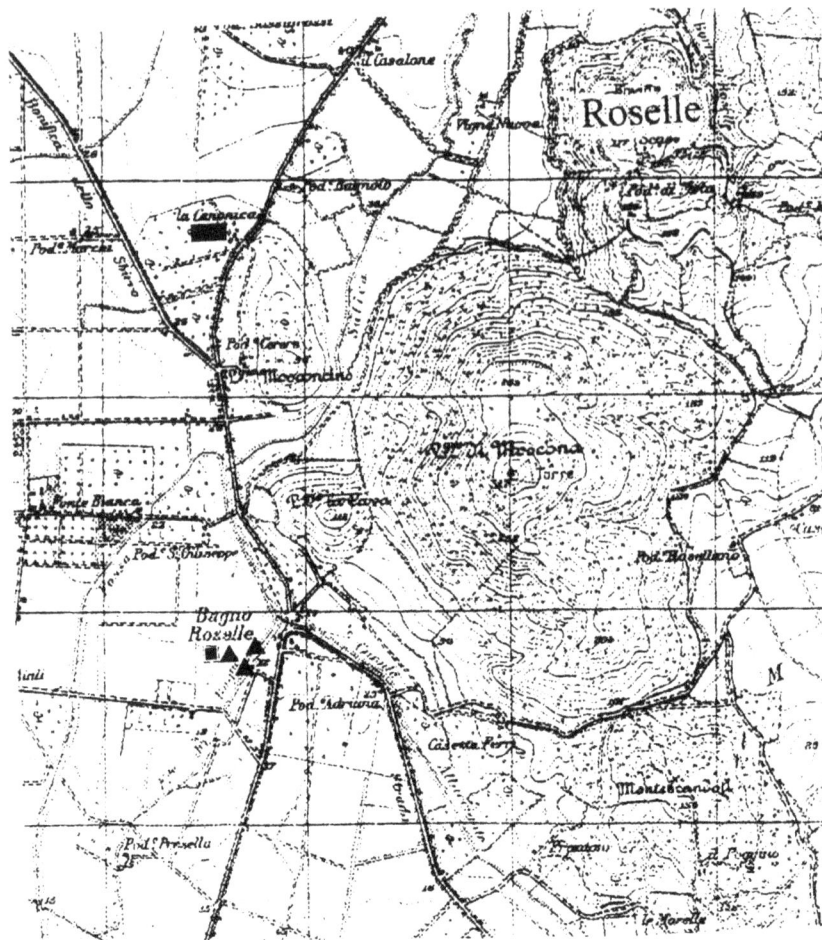

**Fig. 12 (see also fig.24). The territory around *Roselle*. (After Gelichi 1999).**

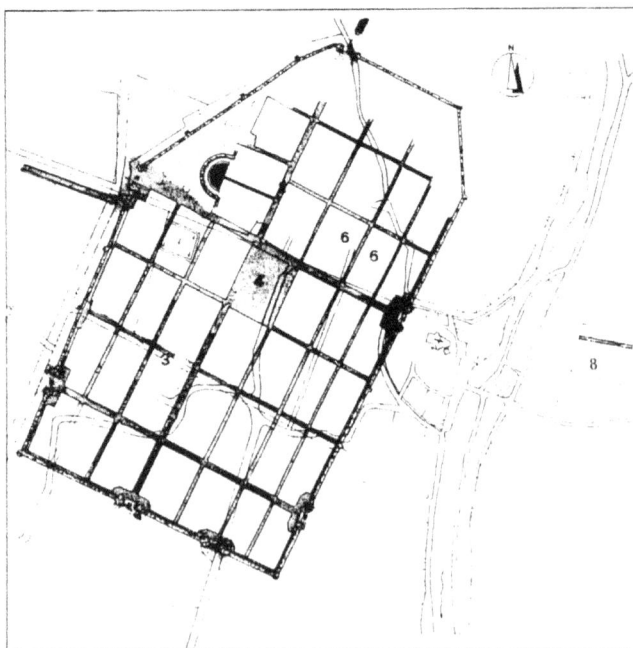

1. *Decumanus maximus*
2. *Kardo maximus*
3. *Canale artificiale*
4. *Foro*
5. *Teatro*
6. *Fabbrica di frecce*
7. *Ponte romano*
8. *Sepolcreto tardo-antico e strada rom*

**Fig. 13. Map of ancient *Iulia Concordia* (6. arrows factory; 8. Late-Antique burial ground and Roman street). (After Croce Da Villa 1987).**

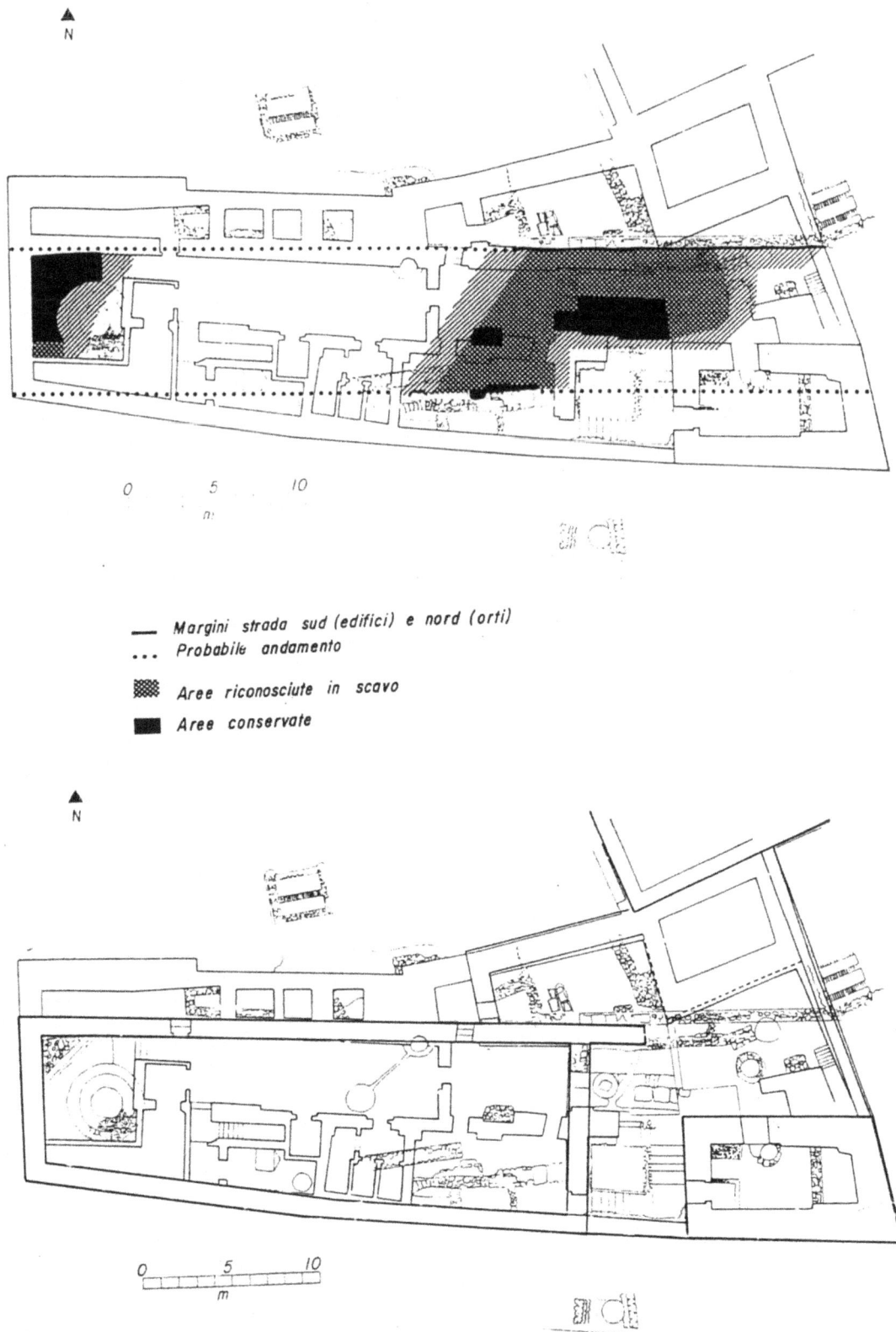

Fig. 14. *Pistoia*. Part of the main East-West Street (first to eleventh century AD) before and after it had been encumbered by episcopal complex's first building (fall of the 11th century AD); (*margini strada…*=borders of the street [buildings southwards, gardens northwards] survived; *probabile andamento*=probable lay-out; *aree conservate*=original parts survived and archaeologically surveyed). (After Vannini 1985).

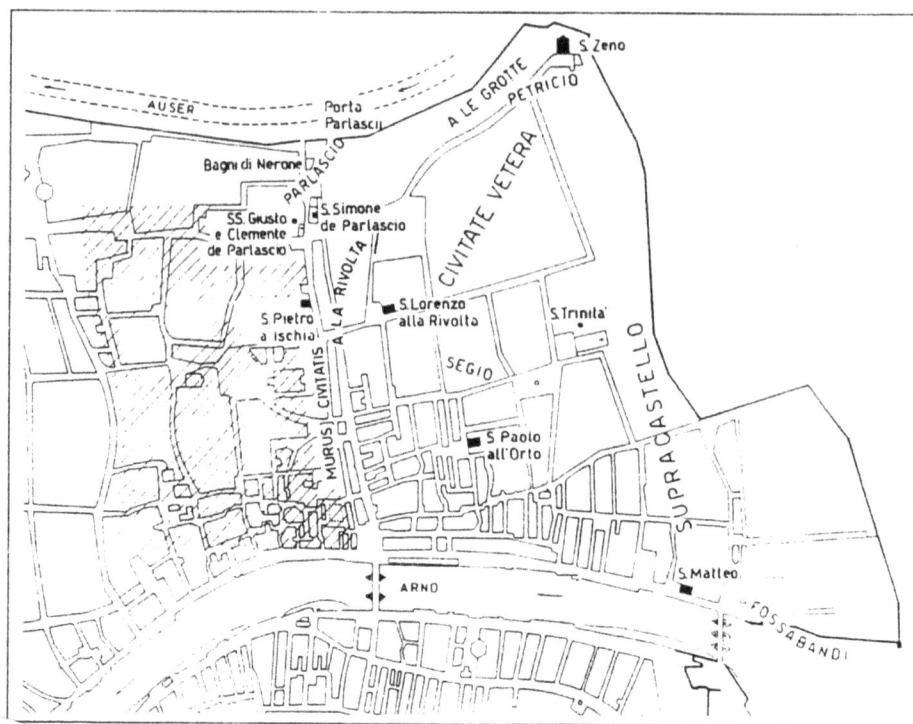

**Fig. 15. Early Medieval *Pisa* (the hatched area is that one enclosed by the city-walls attested to among early-11th-century sources). (After Garzella 1990).**

**Fig. 16. Late Antique and Early Medieval towns of the Region of *Abruzzi*. (After Giuntella 1994).**

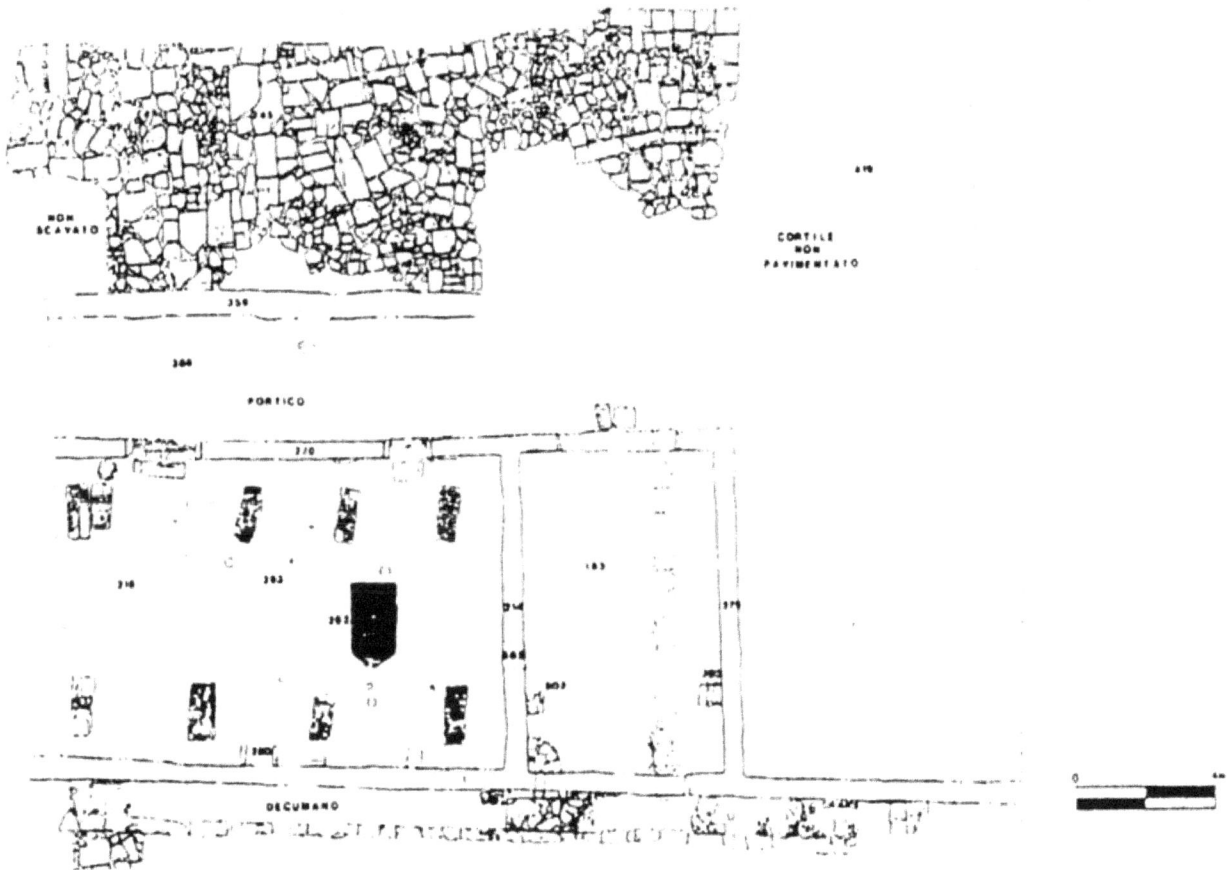

Fig. 17. *Brescia, via Alberto Mario* (Street). Gothic-Age building (*non scavato*=not excavated; *cortile non pavimentato*=not paved courtyard); ruler: 0 - 6ft. 7"/2 m. (After Brogiolo – Gelichi 1998).

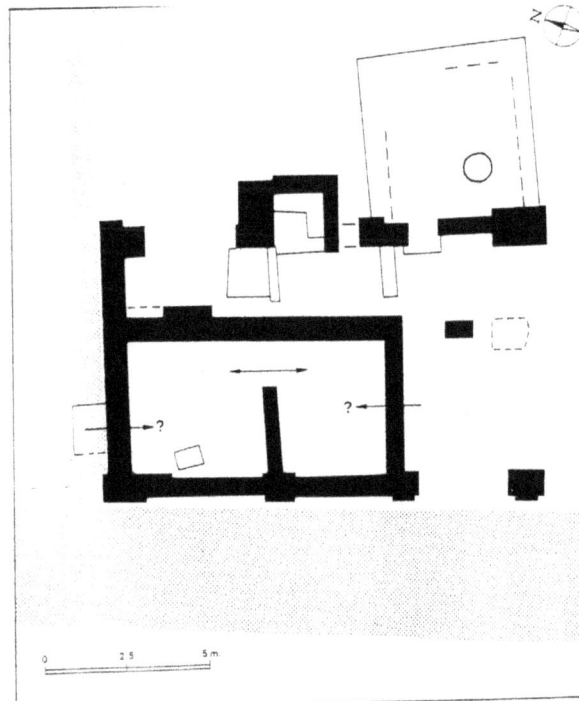

Fig. 18. *Classe, RA (Podere Chiavichetta)*. Hypothetically reconstructed plan of the building readjusted out of the previous store house n. 2. Ruler: 0 – 1 rd. (5 ½ yd.)/5 m. (After Ortalli 1991).

Fig. 19a. Interior walls masonry of the Byzantine *castrum* at *St. Antonino di Perti* (*SV*). (After Cagnana 1994).
Fig. 19b. *Luni* (*SP*). Ground-works of the Byzantine cathedral in *opus spicatum* (herringbone technique), built
with big schistose stones. (After Cagnana 1994).

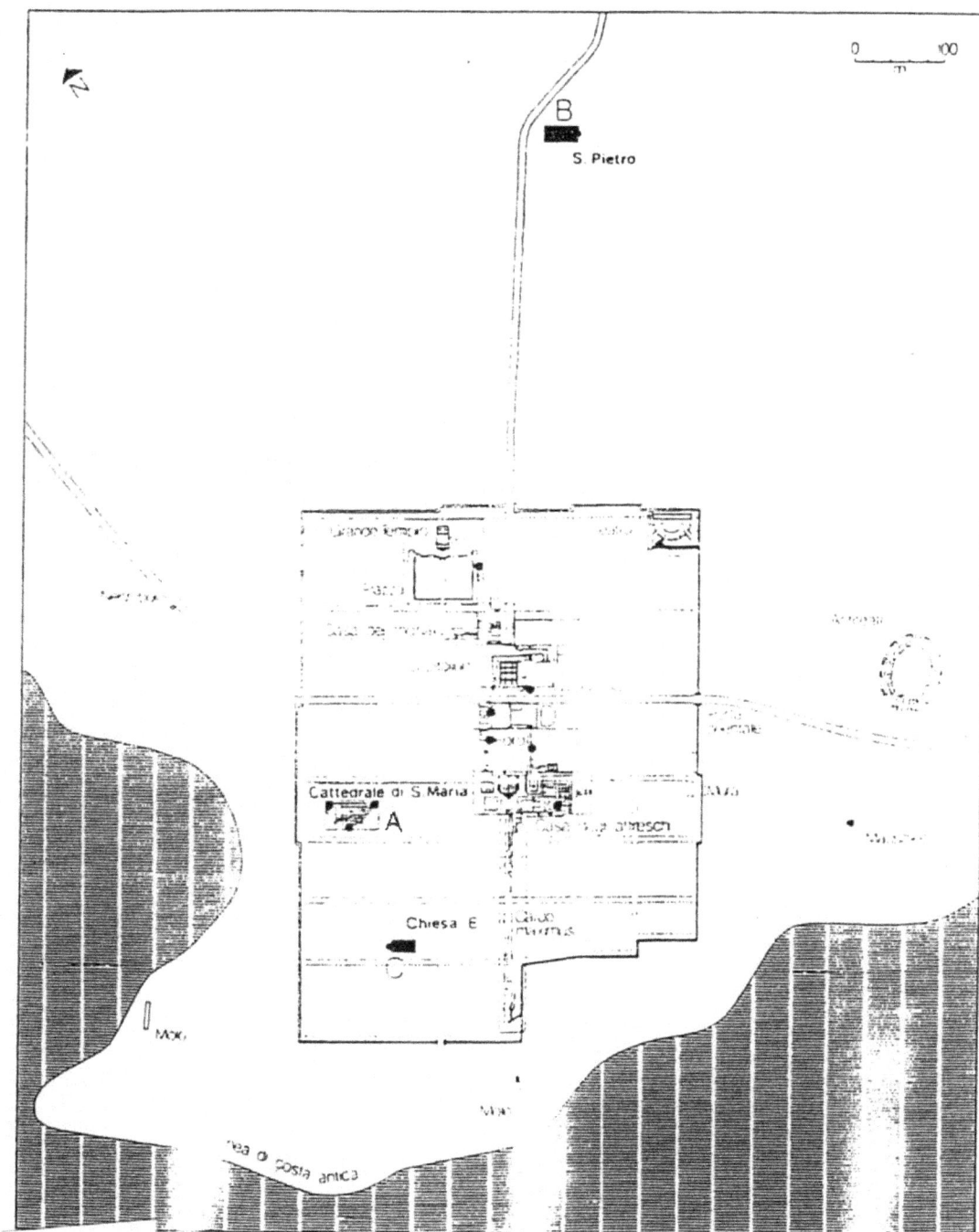

**Fig. 20.** *Luni* (*SP*)**. Map of the Byzantine and Early Medieval town (A=St. Mary's Cathedral). Ruler: 0 – 110 yd./100 m. (After Gandolfi 1998).**

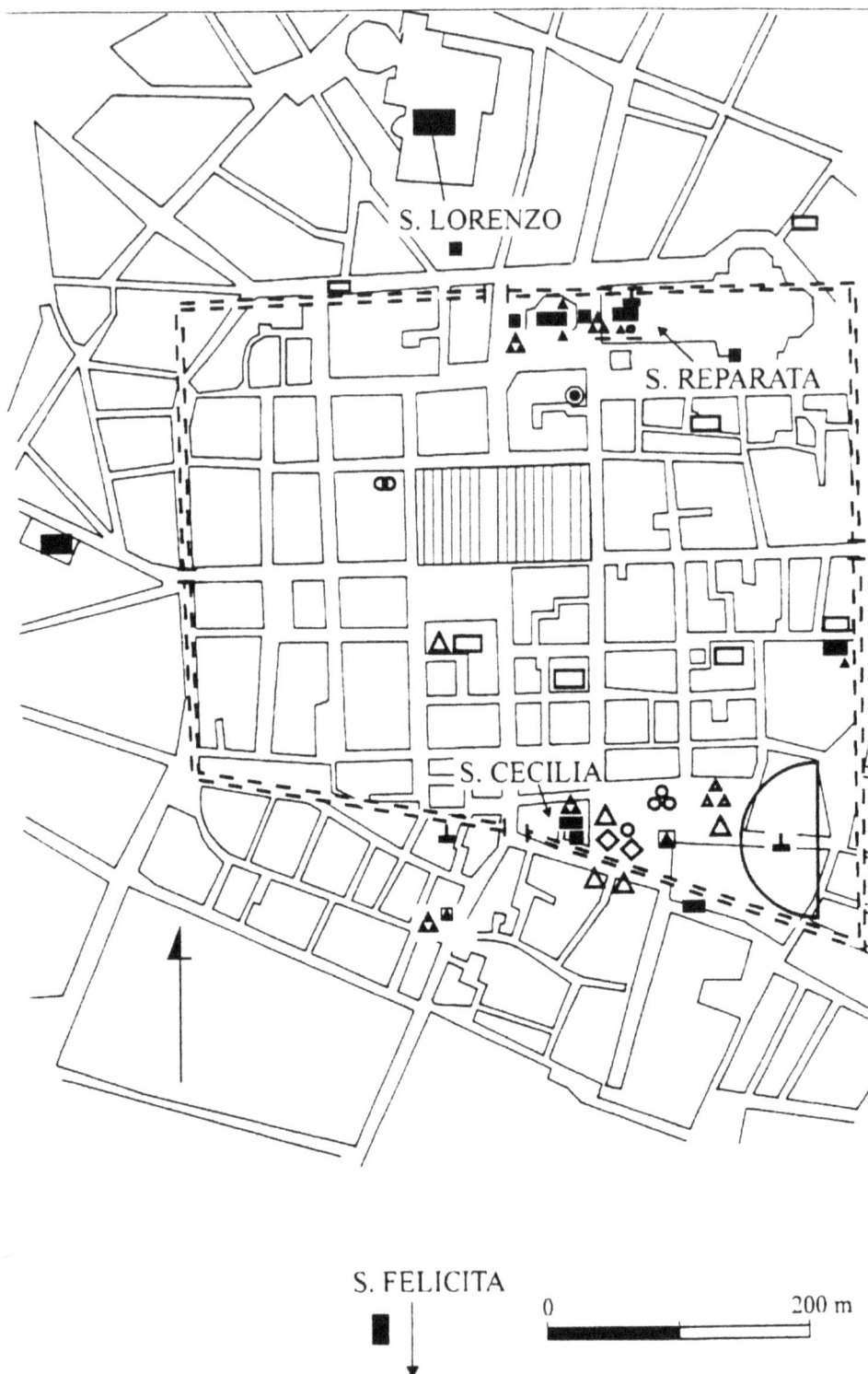

**Fig. 21 (see also fig.24). Map of Early Medieval Florence (the area of *St. Giovanni* up to the right). Ruler: 0 – 220 yd./200 m. (After Gelichi 1999).**

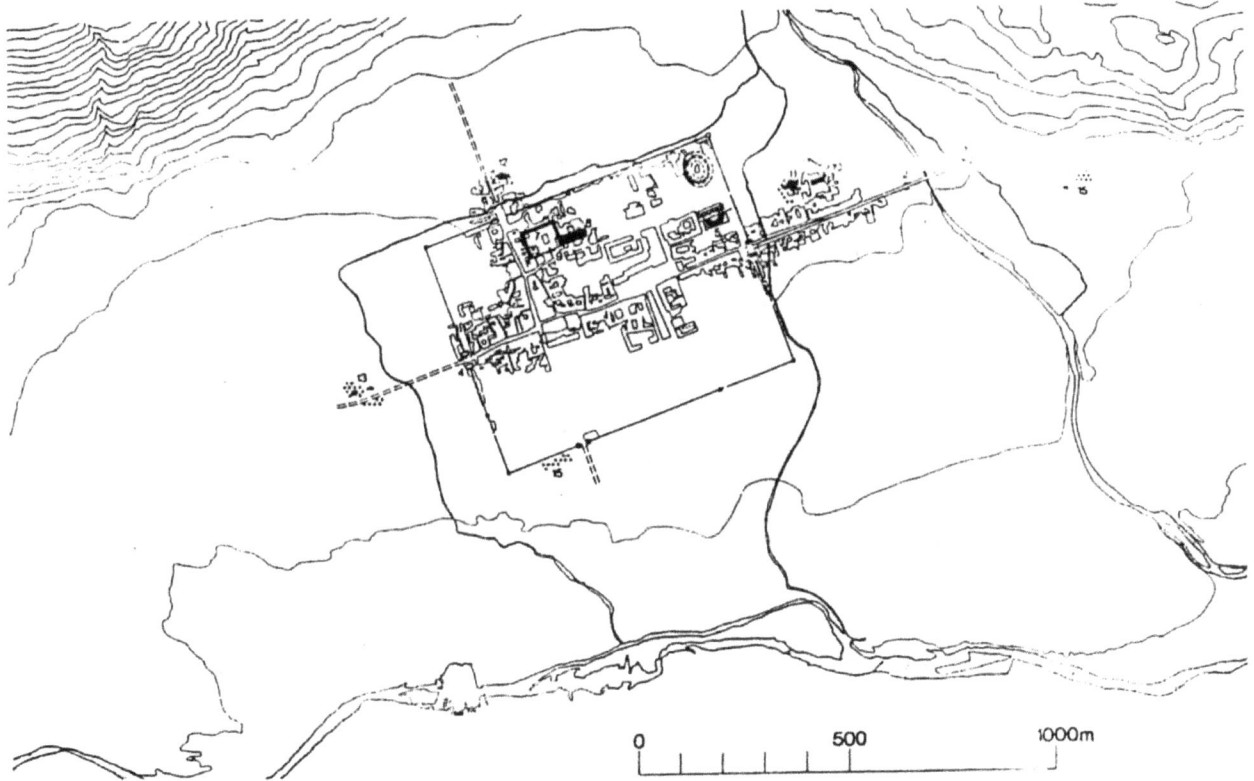

Fig. 22. Map of the Town of *Aosta*. In particular: *Augustus'* Arch (2); *Porta Praetoria* (3); Cathedral (8); *St. Lorenzo*'s Church (11); *necropoles* (15). Ruler: 0 – 5 fur. (5/8 sta. mi.)/1000 m. (After Perinetti 1989).

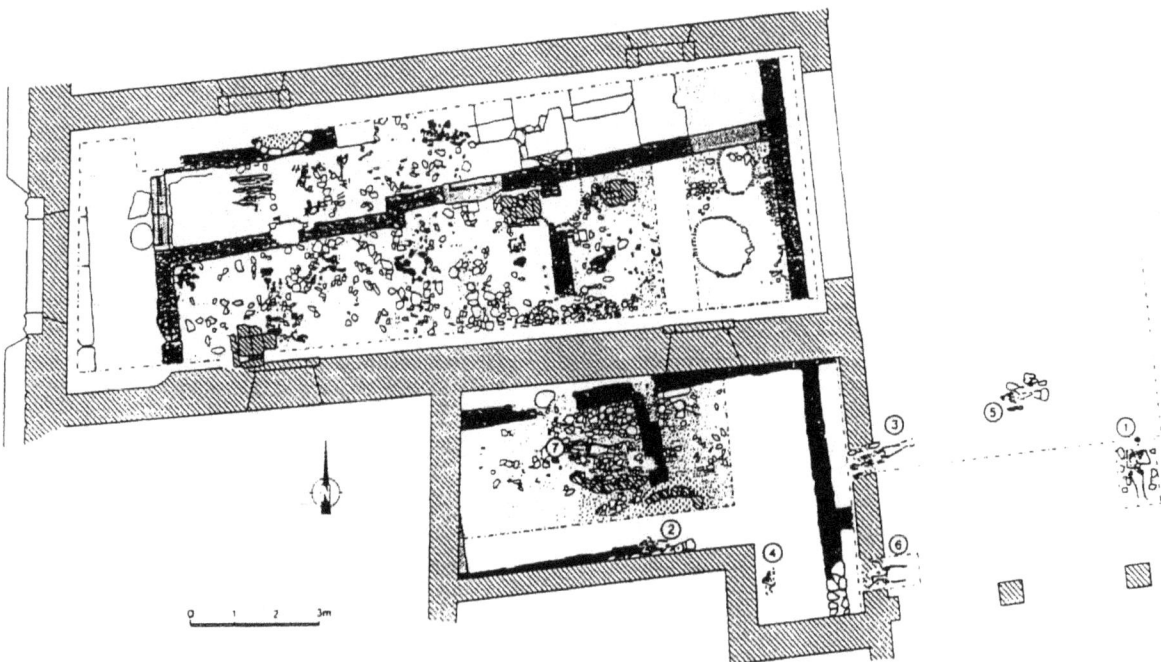

Fig. 23. *Trent, Palazzo Tabarelli*. Late Antique and Early Medieval phases: dwelling houses and burials' location. Ruler: 0 – c. 10 ft./3 m. (After Cavada 1998).

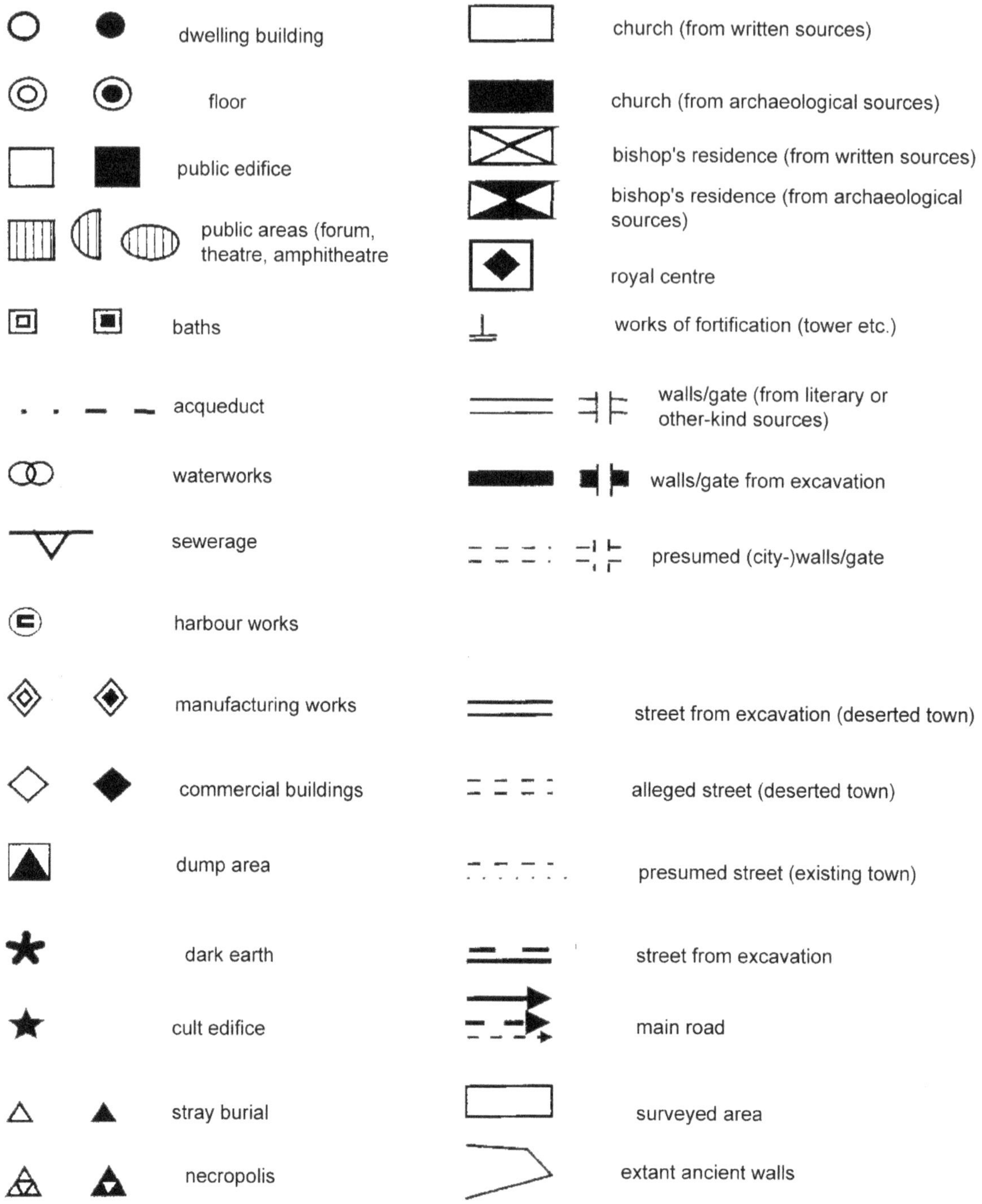

| | | |
|---|---|---|
| ○ ● | dwelling building | □ church (from written sources) |
| ◎ ◉ | floor | ■ church (from archaeological sources) |
| □ ■ | public edifice | ⊠ bishop's residence (from written sources) |
| | public areas (forum, theatre, amphitheatre | ⧖ bishop's residence (from archaeological sources) |
| ▣ ▣ | baths | ◈ royal centre |
| · · — — | acqueduct | ⊥ works of fortification (tower etc.) |
| ∞ | waterworks | ═ ⊣ ⊢ walls/gate (from literary or other-kind sources) |
| ▽ | sewerage | ▬ ▪ ┠ walls/gate from excavation |
| ⊝ | harbour works | = = = : presumed (city-)walls/gate |
| ◈ ◈ | manufacturing works | ═ street from excavation (deserted town) |
| ◇ ◆ | commercial buildings | = = = : alleged street (deserted town) |
| ▲ | dump area | - - - - presumed street (existing town) |
| ✳ | dark earth | ═ ═ street from excavation |
| ★ | cult edifice | ═→ main road |
| △ ▲ | stray burial | □ surveyed area |
| ◬ ◬ | necropolis | extant ancient walls |

Empty (prior) and full (later) signs indicate relative chronology (if contemporaneous all of them marked with a full sign); as regards churches and bishop's residences empty sign means from literary sources, while full sign from archaeological data.

**Fig. 24. Legend of symbols (figures 10, 11a, 11b, 12, 21). (After Gelichi 1999).**

www.ingramcontent.com/pod-product-compliance
Lightning Source LLC
Chambersburg PA
CBHW061302270326
41932CB00029B/3443